MPRE
Practice Questions

Practice Questions for the Multistate
Professional Responsibility Examination

Phone (800) 529-2651 • Fax (800) 529-2652

MPRE Practice Questions

Copyright 2013 AmeriBar

ISBN13: 978-1470008185

Table of Contents

MPRE QUESTIONS

MPRE Practice Questions

PRACTICE QUESTIONS

QUESTION #1

An attorney has an active law practice. Many clients of the attorney neither fully nor timely pay the attorney's bills. The attorney cannot, however, withdraw from representing many of them because of their relationship's advanced stage. Consequently, the attorney adds a clause to his standard representation agreement as a proactive measure to prevent this problem in the future. Any new clients would need to execute the agreement before the attorney could begin working for them. The clause provides that the attorney may withdraw from representing the client based on the client's non-payment and/or late payment of the attorney's bills, provided that attorney provides reasonable warning that the attorney will withdraw unless the obligation is fulfilled. The clause permits the clients time to consult with a different lawyer about the agreement before executing it. The clause also provides that the attorney will invoke the clause if the client fails to pay him.

Assuming the attorney does not represent clients in a capacity in which the approval of a judge would be required for withdrawal of legal representation, would it be proper for the attorney to invoke the clause for withdrawal if a new client does not pay the attorney's bills?

A.   No, because withdrawal is never warranted simply because a client fails to pay the attorney's bills.

B.   No, because the clause does not allow the client time to consult with a different lawyer about the agreement   before executing it.

C.   Yes, because the clause gives the client notice that the attorney will invoke the clause if he does not receive payment.

D.   Yes, because the clients expressly agree to the withdrawal by executing the agreement.

QUESTION #2

A plaintiff hires an attorney to pursue a tort cause of action against a defendant. The plaintiff receives a satisfactory award of damages after pretrial mediation of the case. The plaintiff forwards to the attorney the entire amount due for services rendered by the attorney, up through obtaining the award.

Following that final event of their attorney-client relationship, a state agency contacts the attorney. The agency requests that the attorney complete and return a detailed financial disclosure form regarding the mediation award. When the attorney notifies the plaintiff of the agency's request, the plaintiff directs the attorney not to comply with it. State law does not require completion by the form by the attorney.

Will it be proper for the attorney to complete and return the form to the agency?

A.   No, unless the attorney considers his compliance to be in the plaintiff's best interest.

B. No, because the plaintiff directed the attorney not to complete and return the form.

C. Yes, if the form will not reveal the attorney's work product.

D. Yes, because the attorney's representation of the plaintiff ended a while ago.

QUESTION #3

An attorney agrees to represent a plaintiff in a discrimination action. The attorney files a civil rights complaint against a defendant in a federal district court. Before trial, Congress repeals the federal statute upon which the complaint is based. On behalf of the defendant, a lawyer files a motion alleging that existing law does not warrant the claims in the complaint due to the statute's repeal, which the motion properly documents. In less than 21 days after the motion is filed, the attorney properly amends the complaint to substitute other valid federal civil rights law for the former statute. Existing law governs the case, not the law existing when the complaint was filed.

Will the attorney be subject to a litigation sanction?

A. No, unless the attorney knew that the repeal of the statute was being debated at the time that the original complaint was filed.

B. No, because the attorney appropriately amended the complaint within 21 days after filing the motion.

C. Yes, unless the attorney disclosed the statute's repeal to the plaintiff before the complaint was filed.

D. Yes, because the attorney's should have premised the original complaint upon the other valid federal civil rights law.

QUESTION #4

A state agency in charge of state employment hires an attorney to develop and implement an employee handbook for all employees of the state. Three years after the attorney completes the handbook, the state discharges an employee for violating a handbook provision. The employee seeks to retain the attorney to sue the department for wrongful discharge. The attorney recalls that when developing and implementing the handbook, the state's attorney general issued an opinion (for internal use only) that authorized discharges on grounds similar to those that were used against the employee. Although at that time the attorney disagreed in writing with the opinion, he had to incorporate into the handbook the attorney general's grounds that the employee allegedly violated. The attorney thinks that the grounds for his disagreement and his awareness of it could improve the employee's prospects of getting reinstated by the department or increase her potential for prevailing in a lawsuit against the department.

It would be proper for the attorney to:

A. Reject the employee as a client but reveal to her the basis for his disagreement with the attorney general.

B. Reject the employee as a client and not reveal to her the basis for his disagreement with the attorney general.

C. Accept the employee as a client only in a lawsuit against the department without revealing the basis for his disagreement with the attorney general.

D. Accept the employee as a client and seek to get her reinstated by revealing the basis for his disagreement with the attorney general.

QUESTION #5

An attorney and a client execute a representation agreement regarding the attorney's handling of the client's divorce action against a defendant. The client agrees that if she is awarded alimony and child custody, she would transfer title to certain real property to the attorney. The case advances to trial. The client receives alimony and child custody by judicial order. The client transfers title to the real property to the attorney.

Does the execution of the representation agreement subject the attorney to discipline?

A. No, because the client received alimony and child custody.

B. No, because the attorney and the client voluntarily executed the representation agreement.

C. Yes, because the attorney entered into a contingency fee agreement.

D. Yes, because the client's real property was improperly subject to the attorney's proprietary interest.

QUESTION #6

An attorney belongs to the state bar. She pays a corporation to broadcast a television advertisement of her services in the state. The advertisement states that she has a perfect trial win record. However, the attorney did lose a trial, although she prevailed on appeal of that case.

Will the attorney be subject to discipline?

A. No, because the advertisement is proper under the rules of professional conduct.

B. No, because the advertisement is protected by principles of constitutional freedom of speech.

C.   Yes, because the advertisement is not protected by principles of constitutional freedom of speech.

D.   Yes, because the advertisement is improper under the rules of professional conduct.

QUESTION #7

A builder enters into an enforceable contract with an owner to construct a home. A judge's wife owns and operates an interior design business. The wife enters into a valid agreement with the owner to decorate the home. While the wife is performing her agreement, the owner files a breach of contract action against the builder in the court where the judge works. The owner gives a gift to the judge that is not part of the wife's compensation under the agreement.

Will it be proper for the judge to accept the gift?

A.   No, if the gift was incident to the wife's business and could reasonably be perceived as intended to influence the judge in his performance of his judicial duties.

B.   No, unless the owner gave the same gift to the builder.

C.   Yes, because the owner does not have a direct business relationship with the judge.

D.   Yes, because a judge can accept gifts from anyone.

QUESTION #8

An attorney duly commences a plaintiff's lawsuit against a defendant. A lawyer agrees to represent the defendant in that lawsuit, and timely files an initial responsive pleading. Pursuant to the jurisdiction's court rules, the lawsuit is subject to mandatory pre-trial mediation. The plaintiff's attorney prevails in her motion to adjourn the scheduled mediation for 30 days. The defendant's lawyer timely files a mediation summary in advance of the rescheduled mediation date. The plaintiff's attorney fails to either notify the plaintiff to attend the mediation or file a mediation summary. Neither the plaintiff's attorney nor the plaintiff appear as required for the mediation session. Consequently, the court clerk properly enters a default against the plaintiff and serves the attorney with a notice of default.

Although the plaintiff's attorney promises the plaintiff that she will get the default set aside, the plaintiff's attorney instead goes on a 30-day vacation and does nothing to address the default. The defendant's lawyer subsequently prevails on a motion for a default judgment against the plaintiff. After the vacation, the plaintiff's attorney files a motion to set aside the default judgment. The motion alleges that the attorney has good cause and a meritorious defense for not participating in mediation. The court denies the motion. The plaintiff does not authorize the attorney to pursue the case any further.

Will the attorney be subject to discipline?

A. No, if she pays the plaintiff the cause of action's fair market value.

B. No, because the court should have granted the motion to set aside the default judgment.

C. Yes, unless the court should have granted the motion to set aside the default judgment.

D. Yes, because she failed to make the required filing of a mediation summary or a motion to set aside the default, and did not move to set aside the default judgment until after her vacation.

QUESTION #9

An attorney only practices transactional law. The attorney has no partners and is not associated with any other lawyers. On a monthly basis, the attorney runs radio spots. They broadcast that her: "office exclusively handles transactional matters, including foreign contracts." An individual hears the attorney's radio spot, and they meet to discuss representation. The attorney conducts a typical client-screening interview with the individual. At its conclusion, the attorney states that:

"Unfortunately, my case load is at its highest level ever. Your requested enforcement of a foreign contract could be rather complex. I would like to recommend a different attorney who also handles foreign contract matters and who might have time to represent you. I strongly suggest that you meet with a different attorney soon in order to preserve your right to enforce the foreign contract."

The individual declines the attorney's offer of a referral, and leaves the office quite discouraged that she was unavailable. About a half year later, the individual locates a different transactional lawyer that deals with foreign contracts. At that time, this lawyer advises that the foreign country's statute of limitation for enforcing the contract expired nearly three months after the individual's meeting with the attorney.

Will the attorney be subject to civil liability?

A. No, because the attorney complied with the relevant rules of professional conduct and acted reasonably with respect to declining the representation.

B. No, because the attorney had the right to declined representation of the individual.

C. Yes, because the attorney's advertisement was false and misleading.

D. Yes, because the attorney failed to provide notice of the foreign country's statute of limitation.

QUESTION #10

A plaintiff retains an attorney to bring a negligence lawsuit against a defendant. Although the plaintiff's cause of action lacks any legal foundation, the plaintiff seeks to waste the defendant's time and funds in defending it. The attorney's complaint incorporates and is premised upon the plaintiff's misrepresentations of fact. The attorney is unaware of the plaintiff's misrepresentations.

When the case goes to trial, the plaintiff gives testimony conforming to the complaint's factual allegations. The judge renders a decision in favor of the plaintiff. Following the entry of an order of judgment, the plaintiff sends the attorney a "confidential" fax confessing that he had initially made false statements of fact and repeated them on the witness stand at trial.

The defendant submits a grievance to the professional authority alleging that the attorney used the plaintiff's trial testimony while knowing of its falsity. Consequently, the disciplinary authority commences disciplinary proceedings against the attorney.

Will it be proper for the attorney to present the plaintiff's fax as part of his defense in the disciplinary proceedings?

A.   No, because the plaintiff revealed what he did in a confidential fax.

B.   No, because the plaintiff could be prosecuted for perjury if the confidential fax is revealed.

C.   Yes, because disclosure of the fax is needed for the attorney's defense.

D.   Yes, because the plaintiff's testimony did not perpetrate a fraud on the judge.

QUESTION #11

An attorney belongs to the bar of her home state. In another state, the attorney maintains a physician's license. The attorney knowingly makes a misrepresentation of a material fact in her physician's license renewal form.

Will the attorney be subject to discipline by the bar in her home state for the misrepresentation?

A.   No, because her conduct did not occur while serving as an attorney.

B.   No, because her conduct did not occur in her home state.

C.   Yes, because her false statement constituted dishonest conduct.

D.   Yes, only if she is convicted of a crime in the other state.

QUESTION #12

A defendant hires an attorney to defend her in a criminal case. The attorney informs her that he expects the cost of representation to exceed the amount of her initial deposit. Without the defendant's knowledge, her grandfather gives the attorney a $500 check with directions to credit it against the costs of defense. The grandfather's only request is that the attorney not inform the defendant about the check because she had told him to "stay out of her life." The attorney applies the $500 towards the balance due from the defendant.

Will it be proper for the attorney to keep and use the grandfather's check?

A.   No, because someone other than the defendant cannot fund her defense.

B.   No, because the attorney lacks the defendant's informed consent to use the funds for her defense.

C.   Yes, because the grandfather has not tried to affect the attorney's handling of the defense.

D.   Yes, because the attorney has not decreased his costs based on the grandfather's payment.

QUESTION #13

An attorney and a client execute a valid retainer agreement that automatically renews from year to year. It provides that the attorney will charge the client $150 per hour for the attorney's services and $75 per hour for his paralegal's services. These amounts are reasonable rates in comparison to the average hourly rates in the jurisdiction where the attorney practices law. After the first year, the attorney increases those hourly rates to $175 and $100, respectively. The attorney does not communicate this change to the client, although the attorney bases the client's bills in the second year on the new hourly rates. The client continues to use and pay for the services of the attorney and the paralegal during the second year of their agreement.

Will the attorney be subject to discipline?

A.   No, because the $25 hourly increases were reasonable.

B.   No, because the retainer agreement obligated the client to pay the hourly rates.

C.   Yes, because the retainer agreement was in writing.

D.   Yes, because the attorney failed to obtain the client's consent to the changed hourly rates.

QUESTION #14

An attorney works for a retail corporation, which is experiencing unexplained discrepancies between its sales records and cash receipts. As the corporation's counsel, the attorney seeks to determine the cause of these discrepancies. She believes that they may be attributable to theft by a cashier, who works for the corporation. The cashier handles and collects the daily cash register returns. The attorney plans to question the cashier about the situation. The attorney does not want to reveal that she considers the cashier responsible for the discrepancies. The attorney intends to falsely tell the cashier that she is not being accused of taking cash and that any answers that she provides are confidential. The attorney intends to use the answers she provides against her in any related proceedings against the cashier.

Will the attorney be subject to discipline for conducting this questioning?

A.   No, because no impending legal proceedings existed against the cashier.

B.   No, because the attorney failed to provide the cashier with legal advice.

C.   Yes, because the attorney made false statements to the cashier.

D.   Yes, unless the attorney instructs the cashier to retain a lawyer before the questioning occurs.

QUESTION #15

An attorney works for a state's law enforcement department. The attorney handles a major consumer fraud case during the last year she works for the department. As lead counsel, she works on the discovery, litigation, and appellate phases of that case concerning a telemarketing investment scheme perpetrated by a telemarketing corporation. The corporation defrauded thousands of people of substantial amounts of money including the life savings of many of the victims. Pursuant to state law, the department makes certain data that the attorney gathered when working on the case available to the public.

The final judgment in the department's favor enjoins the corporation's domestic operations, but does not enjoin the corporation's foreign operations. This judgment imposed substantial punitive fines against the corporation.

Pursuant to the controlling law, individuals can bring their own actions against the corporation for damages arising from its fraudulent activities.

The attorney opens her own law office after leaving the department. Five individuals file separate actions against the corporation alleging damages from its fraudulent activities attributable to the foreign operations. The corporation contacts the attorney seeking her representation in those actions.

Will the attorney be subject to discipline by defending the corporation in these private actions?

A.   No, because of the attorney's particular knowledge of this type of law.

B.   No, because certain data gathered by the attorney is now available to the public.

C.   Yes, because the final judgment is completely dispositive of the corporation's liability.

D.   Yes, because of the attorney's substantial responsibility in the department's case against the corporation.

QUESTION #16

An attorney enters into a valid contingency fee agreement to represent a client in a legal malpractice lawsuit. Their agreement awards the attorney 15% of the recovery in a trial and 10% of the recovery from a settlement. The total legal fee cannot be greater than $75,000. The attorney is does not have much trial experience. The attorney contacts a trial lawyer seeking assistance in the event that the case goes to trial. The client provides written consent to the arrangement with the trial lawyer following complete disclosure. Pursuant to the fee contract between the attorney and the trial lawyer, the trial lawyer associates with the attorney because of his special competence with trial of legal malpractice matters based on training and past experience. The attorney and the trial lawyer reasonably estimate that the attorney will provide a majority of the work if the case settles before trial, and that the trial lawyer would provide a majority of the work if the case goes to trial.

The fee contract between the attorney and the trial lawyer provides:

"This matter's entire fee is fifteen percent of the recovery in a trial and ten percent of the recover from a settlement, with a total fee not greater than $75,000. The attorney will participate in pre-trial work and be the client's contact person. The trial lawyer will develop the case and try the case if no settlement occurs. The fee will be split as follows: 1) If the case settles - 70 percent to the attorney and 30 percent to the trial lawyer; 2) If the case goes to trial - 30 percent to the attorney and 70 percent to the trial lawyer"

Will the attorney and the lawyer be subject to discipline for their fee-splitting arrangement?

A.   No, because the fee split between them seems proportionate to the work each actually did.

B.   No, because the entire fee amount is the same as in the agreement between the client and the attorney.

C.   Yes, because the client provided written consent.

D.   Yes, because the attorney cannot present the case at trial.

QUESTION #17

Three attorneys form a law firm. These attorneys only practice law in their home state. Unlike a neighboring state, the home state does not require mandatory continuing legal education. Accordingly, at the partners' monthly meeting, two attorneys vote not to include continuing legal education courses as an expense that the firm will reimburse. After casting his dissenting vote, the dissenting attorney declares that he will not participate in any optional continuing legal education courses because of the firm's policy against reimbursement. The firm maintains malpractice insurance coverage for the attorneys.

Will it be proper for the dissenting attorney not to participate in any continuing legal education courses?

A.   No, because absent the dissenting attorney's participation in those courses, he will not maintain legal competence.

B.   No, because the firm provides malpractice insurance coverage.

C.   Yes, because the dissenting attorney does not practice law in the neighboring state.

D.   Yes, if the dissenting attorney keeps abreast of changes in the law and its practice, and engages in continuing study and education.

QUESTION #18

A corporation's stock is traded on a public stock exchange. Some of the shareholders want to bring a lawsuit against the corporation because they are upset with certain conduct by the corporation's management. An attorney agrees to represent shareholders of a corporation in a derivative action. The attorney properly files the action against the corporation in a civil court. The court clerk places the action on a judge's civil docket. A trust account maintained for the judge owns some shares of publicly traded corporations. Before any pre-trial proceedings commence in the derivative action, the judge checks with the trustee about whether his trust contains any shares of the corporation. The trustee tells the judge that the trust owns a substantial number of shares of the corporation's stock. Only the trustee and the judge know of the stock ownership. The judge goes forward with pre-trial proceedings in the derivative action.

Will the judge be subject to discipline?

A.   Yes, because the judge did not disclose his stock ownership.

B.   Yes, because the judge did not disqualify himself from the case.

C.   No, because the judge holds the shares in a trust, not in direct ownership.

D.   No, because only the trustee and the judge know about the shares.

QUESTION #19

Al Attorney and Barbara Lawyer are members of the state bar. The two attorneys were friends in graduate school where Al obtained his L.L.M. and Barbara obtained her Ph.D. After exclusively practicing bankruptcy law for 10 years at different firms, they form a partnership. The firm places an advertisement in a monthly magazine that is circulated in their home state.

The advertisement states:

Al Attorney, J.D., L.L.M.
Barbara Lawyer, J.D., Ph.D.
Attorney & Lawyer, P.C.
1 Main Ave., City, State, 11111

Phone Number (888) 888-8888.

Will the attorneys be subject to discipline?

A.   Yes, because the appearance of L.L.M. and Ph.D. is superfluous.

B.   Yes, if the firm's practice is restricted to the subject matter in which the degrees of L.L.M. and Ph.D. are needed.

C.   No, because only law is a licensed profession.

D.   No, because they have the degrees referenced.

QUESTION #20

A state administrative agency issues a subpoena to a witness to testify at a hearing. An attorney agrees to represent the witness at the hearing. The attorney counsels the witness that she could exercise a constitutional right not to respond to some questions that the attorney reasonably believes would be against the witness's best interest to answer. The attorney bases this incorrect advice on an overruled Supreme Court decision. The administrative law judge instructs the witness that her failure to answer constitutes a criminal offense for which she would be prosecuted, and informs the attorney of the subsequent Supreme Court decision. Nonetheless, the attorney persists in advising the witness not to testify. Relying on the attorney's repeated counsel, the witness continues to remain silent in response to the questions. As a result, the witness is convicted for not answering the question.

Will the attorney be subject to discipline?

A.   No, because the witness followed the attorney's advice.

B.   No, because the attorney had a reasonable belief that the witness was legally entitled not to answer the question.

C.   Yes, because the attorney's repeatedly incorrect advice shows a lack of preparation on his part.

D.   Yes, because the witness violated the law by heeding the attorney's counsel.

QUESTION #21

An attorney's friend requested that the attorney complete a form provided by a jurisdiction's bar admission authority. The friend would like the attorney to provide a favorable description of her step-cousin's character and fitness to practice law. The friend only briefly sees and visits with her step-cousin once a year. The step-cousin's father, however, has described the step-cousin to the friend as possessing the character traits of truthfulness and diligence. The friend tells the attorney of this description and that the friend believes in its accuracy. The attorney met the friend's step-cousin at a gathering and found her to appear truthful and honest. The attorney, based on the experience at the gathering, and trust of her friend's opinion, completes the form favorably.

Unbeknownst to the attorney and the friend, the step-cousin was involved in a plan to embezzle money from his former employer, for which he entered a plea deal.

Will the attorney be subject to discipline for filling out the form?

A.   No, because the attorney reasonably believed the friend's representations.

B.   No, unless the attorney learns of the step-cousin's involvement in the plan and does not notify the proper authority.

C.   Yes, because he should have completed his own investigation into step-cousin's character.

D.   Yes, because by completing the form the attorney misrepresented the facts.

QUESTION #22

A district attorney handles the prosecution of an accused for stealing a car from a dealership's inventory lot. The accused refutes the charges on the basis that she was at her boyfriend's residence when the alleged offense occurred. An employee, who works for the dealership, provides trial testimony. The employee testifies that he recognized the accused's picture in a photographic array, which a police officer showed to him. The district attorney presents a recording of the employee's 911 call reporting the event and describing the accused and the car. The judge renders a judgment of conviction and sentences the accused for the offense. After the trial, the accused's lawyer discovers additional evidence that the employee initially picked another person's photograph from the photographic array before the police officer suggested the accused's picture to him. The accused's lawyer learns that the district attorney knew of that evidence, but failed to reveal it to the lawyer. The lawyer's pretrial discovery request did not seek such evidence.

Will the district attorney be subject to discipline?

A. No, because the lawyer failed to make a pretrial discovery request for that type of information.

B. No, because the district attorney did not have to initially disclose the additional evidence that was later discovered.

C. Yes, because the judge could have identified the accused based on the 911 call recording.

D. Yes, because the subsequently discovered evidence tended to negate the accused's culpability for the offense.

QUESTION #23

A defendant is called to testify before a legislative committee. The defendant provides testimony before the committee under oath, subject to the penalty of perjury, without being represented by counsel. The defendant is subsequently charged with perjury allegedly arising from that testimony. After an attorney agrees to represent the defendant in the perjury prosecution, the defendant informs the attorney that she made fraudulent statements in her testimony before the committee.

The attorney will be subject to discipline if he:

A. fails to provide notice of the fraudulent statements to the police.

B. provides notice of the fraudulent statements to the police.

C. remains the defendant's counsel.

D. remains the defendant's counsel unless the defendant admits her fraudulent statements.

QUESTION #24

A partner attorney, a partner in a law firm, specializes in antitrust law. A conglomerated company hires the partner attorney's firm in response to receiving a government notice to cease and desist from violating antitrust law. Although the partner attorney agrees to represent the company, another existing case that she was handling unexpectedly was set for trial at an imminent time after an anticipated settlement did not occur. Because that trial would bring the firm more revenue than the company's case, the partner attorney transfers the company's case to an associate lawyer in the firm.

The associate lawyer objects to this new assignment based on his ignorance of antitrust law. He also states that he lacks reasonable time to gain sufficient legal competence to handle the company's case without the partner attorney's assistance. The partner attorney replies that her caseload prevents her from assisting him and that she believes he can handle this assignment.

Did the partner attorney properly handle this case?

A. No, because of the partner attorney's awareness that the associate lawyer lacked the competence to handle the case and her failure to provide adequate oversight to ensure the company's protection.

B. No, because the partner attorney lacked the company's consent to transfer its case to the associate lawyer.

C. Yes, because the associate lawyer's license to practice law qualified him to handle any type of case.

D. Yes, because the partner attorney could withdraw from any case if handling it would cause her substantial financial hardship.

QUESTION #25

A defendant meets with an attorney and requests representation as defense counsel against charges of being a minor in possession of controlled substances. In the state where the defendant is charged with this offense, a minor is a person less than 21 years old. The defendant informs the attorney that her state identification card indicates that she is 22 years old. The defendant admits to the attorney that she has a fake identification card, but asks the attorney not to reveal her true date of birth at the trial on the charged offense. The defendant states that she would not reveal her true date of birth as a trial witness. The attorney advises that, in order to provide a valid defense, the defendant must take the witness stand at trial. When the attorney asks the defendant what is her date of birth, she gives the date on the fake identification card. The attorney does nothing in response to this answer.

Will the attorney be subject to discipline?

A. No, because the attorney became aware of the defendant's real date of birth through representing her.

B. No, because the defendant's real date of birth was not an issue in the proceeding.

C. Yes, because the attorney used the defendant's date of birth in defense of the case while knowing of its falsity.

D. Yes, because the defendant violated the law by using a fake identification card.

QUESTION #26

An attorney and a client have a written fee contract. The client agrees to pay an hourly fee that the attorney will invoice monthly. The client must pay each invoice within one month. Each invoice states that delinquent payment or non-payment could result in withdrawal by the attorney.

Four months before the trial of the client's case, the client pays that month's invoice one month late. Three months before the trial, the client fails to pay that month's invoice. Two months before the trial, the client does not pay that month's invoice, which states:

"You made a delinquent payment of an invoice and did not pay the last invoice. If you fail to pay off your account balance pursuant to this invoice, I will move to withdraw from representing you."

One month before the trial, the attorney writes the client a letter stating that he will move to withdraw from the representation if the client does not pay the last invoice within one week. At the end of the week, when the client does not make any payment, the attorney files a motion to withdraw from representing the client with the court.

Will the attorney be subject to discipline?

A. Yes, because the contract is invalid.

B. Yes, because the conduct of the attorney and the client does not support withdrawal.

C. No, because the client's conduct requires withdrawal.

D. No, because the attorney may move to withdraw under these circumstances.

QUESTION #27

A plaintiff and an attorney enter into a contingency fee agreement. The agreement provides the attorney with 20% of the plaintiff's recovery of money damages. Pursuant to the plaintiff's request, the attorney files a trespass lawsuit against a defendant. The defendant's lawyer makes an offer of settlement that the plaintiff accepts. The settlement provides that the defendant would make five equal payments to the attorney of $1,000 in the next five months. Upon receiving the first $1,000 check, the attorney deposits it in her general account and promptly issues a $800 check to the plaintiff.

Will the attorney be subject to discipline?

A. No, because the attorney deposited the check in a proper account because the case is over.

B. No, because the attorney issued the check to the plaintiff in a correct amount.

C. Yes, because the attorney deposited the check in an improper account.

D. Yes, because the attorney issued the check to the plaintiff in an incorrect amount.

QUESTION #28

An attorney, a solo practitioner, undertakes representation of a plaintiff, an individual. The plaintiff brings a complex business law action against a defendant, a major company. The defendant retains a large firm that deluges the attorney with lengthy pleadings and numerous motions. This case involves extensive discovery requiring review of voluminous documents. The plaintiff objects to this pretrial process as being far more time consuming and costly than anticipated. The attorney advises that to reduce this pretrial process would adversely affect the plaintiff's prospects of prevailing. The attorney thinks that the pretrial process must continue for several more months. The attorney believes that the plaintiff must file several motions and serve additional discovery requests, while the plaintiff wants the process to end, and to go to trial as soon as possible. Many other lawyers are available and competent to handle this matter.

Would it be proper for the attorney to seek the trial court's approval to withdraw from representing the plaintiff?

A.   No, because the attorney is obligated to obey the plaintiff's directions.

B.   No, because the plaintiff has not authorized the attorney to withdraw.

C.   Yes, because the attorney is entitled to withdraw from representing the plaintiff at any point before a trial occurs.

D.   Yes, because the plaintiff's demands render it unreasonably difficult for the attorney to competently and effectively represent the plaintiff.

QUESTION #29

A prosecutor charges a defendant with murder. The defendant, a famous athlete, retains an attorney, a high-profile defense counsel. The defendant declines to enter a plea agreement with the prosecutor. The attorney advises the defendant that a trial will be very costly. The defendant states that:

"I could only afford to give you the initial retainer payment. But I cannot pay for any additional fees. I would like to transfer to you any present or future rights that I might have to develop any type of media entertainment from this pending trial and its related circumstances. If you accepted this offer of transfer, no further payment would be required for your legal services for the entire trial."

The attorney responds that:

"Let me think about your proposal. For now, I suggest that you consult with another attorney regarding if such an arrangement would be advantageous to you. You could do that and get back in touch with me in a few days."

The defendant does not consult with another lawyer about the proposal.

Will the defense attorney be subject to discipline?

A. No, because the defendant failed to consult with another lawyer.

B. No, because the murder case is a criminal proceeding rather than a civil proceeding.

C. Yes, because the attorney is not permitted to enter into an agreement giving the attorney literary or media rights of the client.

D. Yes, because the attorney has not completed representing the defendant.

QUESTION #30

A title company and a real estate attorney enter into a contract. The company allows the attorney free use of an office in its main office building. The company permits the attorney to use the office for his private practice under two conditions. First, while using the office, the attorney may not represent any clients that present a conflict of interest to the company. Second, the attorney would assist with work relating to the company's clients for free.

If a company's client needs legal work with respect to a deed or contract, the company's non-lawyer employee would assist that client, and determine if the client needed any legal documents. The employee would tell the client that the company's staff would develop the appropriate document or documents and later present them to the client for signature.

Pursuant to the employee's written instruction regarding the needed documents, the attorney would develop the documents and do all related legal work. The attorney neither met with the company's clients, nor billed them for his work.

Will the attorney be subject to discipline?

A. No, because the attorney does not charge the company's clients for his work.

B. No, because the attorney is not advising the company's clients directly.

C. Yes, because the agreement is restricting the attorney's right to practice law.

D. Yes, because the agreement is causing the attorney to assist the company in the practice of law.

QUESTION #31

A judge is up for election to the state supreme court. Recently, the judge authored a divisive opinion for the state court of appeals. The opinion interprets when the compensation clause of the state constitution allows state government to take private property for public use. That interpretation expands the scope of permissible takings beyond only those that are necessary for public use. The new scope of takings include those that are beneficial for economic development. The judge participates in a public debate with his opponent. They discuss the case about governmental takings of land. The judge says, "I correctly decided the case and I would decide the same way if I hear the case on the Supreme Court." The case is on appeal to the state supreme court.

Will the judge be subject to discipline for that statement?

A.   No, because the judge is exercising the constitutional right of free speech.

B.   No, because the judge has immunity.

C.   Yes, because the statement indicates that the judge will not fairly decide the issue.

D.   Yes, because the judge discussed the topic in public.

QUESTION #32

A company utilizes an attorney as retained outside counsel for almost a decade. A recent change in the company's business affects the company's legal status. The attorney's research discovers that the change arguably renders an existing corporate document on file with a state office misleading and fraudulent. The attorney promptly informs the company's board of directors that the company must change the filing immediately to avoid civil liability. The board rejected the attorney's request to make the change on the basis that the change did not make the filed document misleading and fraudulent. In response to the attorney's threat to cease representing the company, the board asserts that by quitting, the attorney would be indicating that the filing was flawed. The board requested that the attorney remain outside counsel. The board stated that the company's corporate counsel would handle this issue. The attorney wishes to withdraw from representing the company based on his reasonable belief that the filing is unlawful and his lack of comfort with the filing in its present form.

Will it be proper for the attorney to withdraw?

A.   No, because the attorney's withdrawal would indicate that the filing is unlawfully flawed.

B.   No, because the attorney's withdrawal could adversely impact the company's prospects of timely correcting the filing.

C.   Yes, because the attorney can permissively withdraw if the company is persisting in a course of conduct that the attorney reasonably believes, but does not know, is fraudulent.

D.   Yes, because the attorney must withdraw since the company is persisting in a course of conduct that the attorney reasonably believes, but does not know, is fraudulent.

QUESTION #33

A plaintiff's attorney is campaigning to be elected as a trial court judge. A defense lawyer is a solo practitioner in the same jurisdiction that the plaintiff's attorney seeks to serve as a trial court judge. Often they have appeared in the same courtrooms and even litigated cases as representatives of party opponents. In light of the defense lawyer's awareness of how the plaintiff's attorney conducts herself in judicial proceedings, the defense lawyer's opinion is that the plaintiff's attorney lacks a judicial temperament. Both represented opposing litigants in a high-profile local case. After a major hearing, a local television station broadcasts a press conference of the defense lawyer. In the broadcast, the defense lawyer comments on camera that: "I believe that the attorney is the worst candidate for a seat on the trial court bench. She is not qualified to be a judge."

Did the lawyer make proper comments?

A. No, because the comments dishonored the judiciary.

B. No, because lawyers cannot make public remarks about judicial candidates.

C. Yes, because the lawyer was not campaigning to be a trial judge.

D. Yes, because the lawyer reasonably believed what he said about the attorney.

QUESTION #34

A plaintiff, an individual, retains an attorney to pursue a breach of contract action against a defendant, a business. The defendant's corporate counsel files a notice of appearance in the action. Upon the plaintiff's request, the attorney contacts a freelance reporter who agrees to attempt to obtain evidence from the defendant. The freelance reporter is to be compensated for questioning the defendant's contract administrator for a purported "news story." The attorney prepares the reporter to ask about the transaction subject to litigation with the plaintiff. The reporter obtains answers that include crucial evidence supporting the plaintiff's action.

Will the attorney be subject to discipline?

A. Yes, because the attorney should have interviewed the contract administrator.

B. Yes, because the attorney prepared the reporter to ask about the transaction.

C. No, because the attorney fulfilled the plaintiff's request.

D. No, because the answers contained evidence important to the action.

QUESTION #35

The government files a complaint against a defendant in a federal court. The government alleges that the defendant violated federal tax law. The defendant files an answer presenting several complex legal issues. At the close of the case, the judge finds that the parties have not sufficiently developed or explained those issues. The judge wants further legal advice in the matter from an expert in tax law that she knows. The expert lacks any interest in the case.

Will it be proper for the expert to consult the judge?

A. No, unless the parties have provided advance written consent to the expert's advising of the judge.

B. No, unless the judge discloses who the expert is, the subject matter of his advice, and provides the parties with a reasonable opportunity to respond to this advice.

C. Yes, because the expert lacks any interest in the case.

D. Yes, if the judge considers the expert's advice necessary to further the interests of justice.

QUESTION #36

An attorney holds a law license and a real estate agent license in the jurisdiction where she lives. Instead of practicing law there, the attorney works as a real estate agent. Although the attorney could have held inactive status as a member of the bar, she maintains an active bar membership status in the jurisdiction. In relation to a real estate transaction in which the attorney represents a seller, she makes misrepresentations of fact to a buyer regarding a house that is being sold. The buyer prevails in a civil action against the attorney alleging misrepresentation. The attorney loses her appeal of the judgment awarding damages to Buyer.

Will the attorney be subject to discipline?

A. No, because the attorney was not convicted of committing a criminal offense.

B. No, because the attorney acted in the seller's best interest.

C. Yes, because the attorney engaged in a real estate career when her bar membership remained active.

D. Yes, because the attorney made a misrepresentation to the buyer.

QUESTION #37

A bar admissions applicant graduates from a public law school. He requests and receives a packet from his state's professional authority to apply for membership to the state bar. One of the questions that he must answer to complete the application form asks if he has ever been convicted of a criminal offense. The question does not indicate if it applies to either juvenile or adult offenses. Without contacting the professional authority and inquiring if the question applies to either or both types of offenses, the applicant assumes that it only applies to adult offenses. He then answers the question "no" because he was not convicted of any adult offenses. However, the applicant was convicted of multiple juvenile offenses.

Did the applicant properly answer the question?

A. No, because the applicant did not attempt to contact the professional authority to inquire whether the question applied to either or both types of offenses.

B. No, because the applicant knowingly made a false statement of material fact.

C. Yes, because the applicant reasonably believed that the question only applied to adult offenses.

D. Yes, because the applicant knowingly made an accurate statement of material fact.

QUESTION #38

An attorney works for a state social services office for three years. While serving in that position, other employees of the office investigate an accused for suspected child abuse and neglect. The attorney does not participate in that investigation and it is not the subject of media reporting. After leaving the office's employ, the attorney joins a law firm that handles family law matters.

Subsequently, the accused is charged with child abuse and neglect pursuant to the office's investigation. The accused seeks to retain the attorney in responding to those charges. The attorney refuses to accept the accused as a client, but indicates that a partner lawyer, another member of the law firm, might accept him as a client. The partner lawyer reviews the case and accepts the accused as a client. The attorney neither aids the partner lawyer with defending the accused, and is in no way compensated.

Will the partner lawyer be subject to discipline for accepting the representation?

A. No, because the attorney did not assist the partner lawyer with handling the accused's defense or receive any compensation.

B. No, because the attorney lacked involvement in or awareness of the investigation of the accused.

C. Yes, because the attorney worked for the office during its investigation of the accused.

D. Yes, unless the state social services office is immediately contacted and agrees to allow the partner lawyer to accept the accused as a client.

QUESTION #39

A married couple wants to adopt a child. An attorney agrees to assist the couple with adopting a child. During the first month of representation, the couple take various steps to facilitate the adoption that are available without requiring the attorney's involvement. The couple assume that the attorney was also taking the needed steps to prepare for accomplishing their objective. When the couple contacts the attorney for more assistance that is necessary to facilitate the adoption, they discover that he has not done any work for them in over a month. At that time, the attorney returns the couple's retainer and acknowledges that they could select another lawyer. The couple finds and meet with a new lawyer. The couple explains the original attorney's handling of the adoption matter to the new lawyer, but ask that she keep quiet about it because they understand that it resulted from some extenuating circumstances over which the original attorney lacked control. Realizing that the original attorney no longer represents the couple and that the couple needs assistance to complete the impending adoption, the new lawyer agrees to represent the couple. The lawyer does not report the original attorney's conduct to the professional authority.

Will the new lawyer be subject to discipline?

A. No, because the original attorney did not commit professional misconduct.

B. No, because the new lawyer does not have to report the original attorney's conduct.

C. Yes, because the original attorney committed professional misconduct.

D. Yes, because the couple asked the new lawyer not to reveal what they told her.

QUESTION #40

An attorney's practice involves handling civil cases on appeal. She enters into a written retainer agreement with a client. The agreement sets forth the attorney's hourly rate of $150. It also provides for the client's payment of a $1,000 appeal bond. The state appellate court rules require posting of the bond if the court grants leave to appeal. The attorney estimates that it will take her 10 hours to prepare and file a notice of appeal and all papers seeking leave to appeal.

Accordingly, the agreement provides for a total retainer amount of $2,500, which the client provides to the attorney. Upon receiving the client's payment, the attorney places the $2,500 in a client trust account that is separate from her general account. The attorney spends 10 hours preparing the notice of appeal and the pleadings seeking leave to appeal before timely filing them. The attorney informs the client that the court of appeals declined to grant leave to appeal. The client, experiencing financial hardship, requests that the attorney return the entire amount of the retainer payment. The attorney issues a $1,000 check to the client and keeps $1,500 in the client trust account pending a determination of how to dispose of the $1,500.

Will the attorney be subject to discipline?

A. No, because the attorney issued a check in the correct amount, although she could have moved the other funds from the client trust account into her general account.

B. No, because the attorney issued a check in the correct amount, and did not move the other funds.

C. Yes, because the attorney should have issued a check to the client for the entire retainer amount, and brought an action to recover legal fees.

D.   Yes, because the attorney issued a check in the wrong amount, and should have kept the other funds in the client trust account.

QUESTION #41

A father is in a permanent comatose condition. His living will designates his daughter, a federal district court judge, as his first patient advocate. The living will alternatively designates his son as his second patient advocate. The daughter believes that she is qualified to serve as the father's patient advocate. Unlike the son, who is estranged from the father, the daughter has always had a close relationship with the father. She reasonably believes that serving as a patient advocate would not impair her performance of judicial duties. The daughter's main role would involve making decisions regarding the father's health care. Although the son or another family member could challenge the living will's validity, that is improbable. Otherwise, the daughter may not need to participate in legal actions concerning her service as a patient advocate. For purposes of this question, a person designated as a patient advocate by a living will occupies a fiduciary position as a type of personal representative of the patient.

Will it be proper for the daughter to serve as patient advocate?

A.   No, because, as a federal judge, she is prohibited from serving in a fiduciary capacity.

B.   No, because the father's family members could challenge the living will's validity.

C.   Yes, because she has a closer relationship to the father than his son does.

D.   Yes, because she believes that assisting the father in this way would not interfere with her performance of judicial duties.

QUESTION #42

A prosecutor primarily handles cases involving charges of drunk driving. In a high-profile case, a defendant declines the prosecutor's plea agreement proposals and demands a jury trial. The defendant is represented by an attorney, who is well known for successfully defending alleged drunk drivers. The prosecutor seeks to gain an advantage in the pending trial of the defendant's case. The prosecutor believes that if the local media presents some negative publicity about drunk driving, it might cause prospective jurors to be more likely to convict the defendant. The prosecutor contacts some local media outlets and asks them to further investigate and report about the circumstances of the defendant's offense, as well as the negative statistics about, and tragic consequences of, drunk driving. Some of these media outlets comply with her request and publicize such stories prior to jury selection in the prosecutor's case against the defendant. The stories provide negative publicity that biases and prejudices prospective jurors against the defendant, contrary to applicable criminal law.

Will the prosecutor be subject to discipline for making this request?

A.   No, because the media outlets informed the public.

B.   No, because the prosecutor did not directly contact any prospective jurors.

C.   Yes, because the media outlets' publicity did not affect the prospective jurors.

D.   Yes, because using the media for this purpose was unethical.

QUESTION #43

A prosecutor prepares and files an information charging a defendant with homicide. The defendant retains an attorney, who obtains his release from custody on bail. Based on the defendant's evidence and representations, the attorney is convinced that the defendant is innocent and that another person is guilty of the charged offense. The defendant, however, doubts that the prosecutor, the trial court, or a jury, will believe the defense. He asks the attorney to tell him how he can avoid further judicial proceedings and where he can go to escape being apprehended for an offense that he did not commit. The attorney declines to answer these questions and advises the defendant that he should voluntarily participate in all subsequent judicial proceedings and not attempt to escape being apprehended. After the defendant left this meeting with the attorney, he travels out the country without informing anyone of his destination. When the defendant fails to appear as scheduled for trial, the attorney explains to the prosecutor what transpired in his last discussion with the defendant.

Will the attorney be subject to discipline?

A.   No, because the attorney cannot be disciplined as a result of a defendant's conduct.

B.   No, because the attorney advised against the defendant's avoidance of judicial proceedings, and escape from being apprehended.

C.   Yes, because the defendant failed to appear as scheduled.

D.   Yes, because the defendant failed to heed the attorney's advice.

QUESTION #44

An entertainment lawyer represents a client, an actor. A movie company's attorney contacts the entertainment lawyer to negotiate a contract employing the client. The company wants to include the client in a movie. The entertainment lawyer and the attorney conduct negotiations and develop a contract that the client and the company approve and execute. While shooting the movie, the client notices that the company did not furnish the specific type of refreshments that he always consumes on the set. The company informs the client that the contract does not require the company to provide the refreshments. As a result, the client makes arrangements for someone to supply them at the client's own cost. The client brings this situation to the entertainment lawyer's attention.

The entertainment lawyer admits that he should have negotiated for, and obtained for the client, a contract provision requiring the company to provide the refreshments. The entertainment lawyer offers to pay the client the value of the refreshments that should have been furnished under the contract. Although the client could have obtained a greater amount of compensation by suing the entertainment lawyer for legal malpractice, he accepts the entertainment lawyer's offer. The entertainment lawyer prepares, and they both sign, an agreement reflecting this arrangement. The entertainment lawyer does not provide the client with either written advice to obtain advice from separate legal counsel before they made that agreement or an opportunity to obtain such advice. The client does not have such counsel when discussing and signing their agreement.

Did the entertainment lawyer engage in proper conduct?

A.   No, because the entertainment lawyer should have provided the client with a legal opinion regarding the agreement.

B.   No, because of the entertainment lawyer's conduct with respect to the client in formation of the agreement.

C.   Yes, because the client voluntarily entered into the agreement with the entertainment lawyer.

D.   Yes, because of the lawyer's representation of the client in formation of the contract with the company.

QUESTION #45

An attorney works for a state agency's legal department for four years. During that time, she handles consumer protection cases. While there, she is lead counsel in an investigation of a company's deceptive advertising practices. As a result of the investigation, the department files criminal fraud charges against the company. After leaving her position with the department, the attorney goes to work for a law firm. At the firm, she discovers that the company has retained a lawyer, a partner of the firm, to assist the company's counsel in defending the client from the criminal fraud charges resulting from her investigation. Promptly, the firm implements measures to screen the attorney from the partner lawyer's representation of the company, such that the department can ensure that the attorney will not breach her duty of confidentiality. The firm also provides written notice of the screening to the agency.

Will it be proper for the firm, and the partner lawyer, to remain involved in defending the company?

A.   No, because the attorney worked for the department prior to working for the firm.

B.   No, because of the attorney's substantial responsibility for the investigation and consequent charges against the company.

C.   Yes, because the firm's measures will prevent the attorney from disclosing to the lawyer any confidential information that she obtained when working for the department.

D.   Yes, because the attorney is obligated to seasonably reveal any exculpatory evidence to the lawyer.

QUESTION #46

As a sole practitioner who recently became a bar member, an attorney has only one client, Beta, a small business. Pursuant their retainer contract, the attorney does transactional work for the client. The attorney relocates her office. Without the client's knowledge, the attorney develops an advertisement for dissemination. In addition to her name, the advertisement states:

"Announcing the opening of my new office at 111 Office Center, phone number (777) 777-7777. I practice these types of transactional law: contracts, property, partnerships, and corporations. Based on my representation of Beta, a small business, as a client, I can draft, review, and enforce documents regarding those legal subjects.   Contact me for considerate and effective legal representation at reasonable rates."

Will the attorney's be subject to discipline for the advertisement?

A.   No, because the advertisement includes the attorney's name and is truthful.

B.   No, because the advertisement identifies the type of law that the attorney practices.

C.   Yes, because the advertisement states that the attorney represents the client.

D.   No, because the advertisement includes the attorney's address.

QUESTION #47

Under state court rules, each party in a criminal case is only entitled to one continuance as a matter of right. A party must make all other requests for continuances by motion with notice to the other party, which may be granted in a trial judge's discretion. A state trial court judge provides notice to all parties in any criminal proceedings before him that he will only grant a second continuance if the moving party can prove that either the party or the party's counsel will be unavailable on the originally scheduled court date due to death or a life-threatening physical condition. In the judge's opinion, no other grounds are sufficient to merit granting a second continuance. The judge believes that to liberally grant a second continuance would cause unmerited delay and risk violating an accused's constitutional right to a speedy trial. In the state's appellate courts, parties may challenge the judge's decisions made pursuant to this policy.

Is the judge's personal policy on granting second continuances proper?

A.   No, because it is not supported by a legal requirement.

B.   No, because it is not fair to either party when the grounds for granting a second continuance is limited to death or a life-threatening physical condition.

C.   Yes, because the judge implements it using discretion.

D.   Yes, because a party whose motion is denied can challenge this decision on appeal.

QUESTION #48

An attorney agrees to provide legal consultation services to a client. In January, they entered into a written retainer agreement. The agreement provides that, pursuant to the client's written instructions, the attorney could make certain legally required payments on the client's behalf using client funds. In February, the client calls the attorney and explains that she is out of the country for an indefinite period. In March, the client writes the attorney a letter requesting that the attorney use funds enclosed in the letter to pay her estimated income taxes in April. The attorney deposits the funds into the client trust account. On April 15, the attorney uses the client's tax payment funds to pay for overdue office rent payments. The attorney does that because the penalties and interest rates were more than the comparable penalties and interest for overdue income taxes. On April 30, the attorney receives a substantial bequest to him from a decedent's estate. He deposits those funds into his general account. On the same day, the attorney issues checks from that account in sufficient amounts to pay the client's income taxes with interest and penalties. The attorney sends the client's income tax payment with interest and penalties to the government. The client does not object when the attorney subsequently informs her of all of the payments.

Will the attorney be subject to discipline?

A.   No, because the attorney's payments using the client's funds did not adversely affect the client and the attorney thought that the client would not object to the payments.

B.   No, because the client implicitly ratified the conduct by not objecting to it.

C.   Yes, because the attorney's actions resulted in a penalty to the client.

D.   Yes, because the attorney improperly utilized the client's funds for office rent payments.

QUESTION #49

A foreign retail corporation that sells headlights is represented by a litigation attorney in a tort lawsuit alleging interference with contractual relations against a domestic automobile manufacturer. The foreign retail corporation alleges that the domestic automobile manufacturer has been contacting the retailer's largest commercial clients, attempting to persuade them to stop doing business with the foreign retailer. The foreign retailer and domestic automobile manufacturer are both in the automotive industry. Another lawyer, a corporate lawyer, is handling the foreign retailer's application for a certificate of authority to transact business in the state where the domestic automobile manufacturer does business. State law provides for an administrative agency to process this application. The agency's determinations are subject to judicial review by state courts.

Another competitor, a domestic headlight retailer, is also in the automotive industry. The domestic headlight retailer contacts the foreign retailer's litigation attorney requesting representation to challenge the foreign retailer's application for a certificate of authority. The foreign competitor is aware that the foreign retailer is represented by the litigation attorney in the tort lawsuit.

Will representation of the foreign competitor by the litigation attorney be proper?

A.   No, because the retailer is presently being represented by the litigation attorney.

B.   No, if both the tort lawsuit and the application to transact business case could be decided by the same appellate court.

C.   Yes, if neither the application to transact business nor the tort action involve the same factual and legal issues.

D.   Yes, because the application to transact business is an administrative matter, whereas the tort action is a civil action.

QUESTION #50

An attorney runs a television advertisement on the local affiliate of a nationwide television network. He appears in the commercial and says to the viewers:

"Has someone you care about, or have you, been involved in a situation resulting in harm, such as an accident? Call me for a no cost, no obligation consultation about your legal rights and remedies. My toll free number is (800)-888-8888. Let me work to protect your interests."

Will the attorney be subject to discipline for this advertisement?

A.   No, if the attorney's entire statement in the television advertisement is truthful and not misleading.

B.   Yes, because the television advertisement may be broadcast into other jurisdictions where the attorney does not belong to the bar.

C.   Yes, because the attorney does not describe his credentials or similar specifics.

D.   Yes, because the television advertisement is intended to promote more lawsuits.

QUESTION #51

An attorney would like to facilitate her clients' payment of her bills for legal fees. For this purpose, the attorney drafts a client agreement whereby the attorney receives the right to publish a book about the client's case upon accepting representation of the client.

Will it be proper for the attorney to use the agreement?

A.   No, because the agreement grants the right upon accepting representation.

B.   No, because the agreement may not grant any right upon accepting representation.

C.   Yes, because the attorney already has the literary right as a matter of law.

D.   Yes, because the attorney has absolute discretion in contracting with clients.

QUESTION #52

An attorney enters into a written agreement to represent a client in pending litigation. Under the agreement's terms, the client retains the attorney pursuant to an initial retainer payment of $7,000, which is to be applied to the attorney's legal fees and costs. The attorney agrees to provide the client with any unearned remainder of the funds. The agreement requires the attorney to issue regular invoices for services rendered and deduct the amount earned from the client's initial payment. The agreement does not specify if the payment is to be placed in a client trust account or a general account. The agreement did not address when the attorney would deduct the amount earned. The attorney places the funds in a client trust account. The attorney subsequently provides the client with regular invoices stating the balance of the client's initial payment and accurately describing work that the attorney did for the client. The attorney does not deduct any of the client's payment from the client trust account until more than 18 months from when the attorney deposited it. By that time, the attorney concludes representation of the client. The attorney transfers $6,000 (the amount of the attorney's fees in representing the client) to the attorney's general account, and mails the client a check for the remaining balance of $1,000.

Did the attorney engage in proper conduct?

A.   No, because the attorney's failure to withdraw funds as earnings accrued caused an improper commingling of funds.

B.   No, because the attorney received the client's payment of funds for the legal fees and costs in advance.

C.   Yes, because the attorney placed the client's funds in the client trust account.

D.   Yes, because the attorney regularly issued invoices to the client.

QUESTION #53

An attorney mainly practices in the field of contracts law. A person selling a piece of real property hires the attorney to prepare a real estate contract for the property. The attorney and her secretary serve as attesting witnesses for the execution of the property's deed. The buyer acquires the property for use by his partnership. The seller becomes mentally incompetent two years after the execution of the deed. A conservator is appointed to handle the seller's legal and financial affairs. The secretary who witnessed the deed's execution dies.

The buyer retains a litigation lawyer, who files a lawsuit against the conservator as the legal representative of the seller's estate, alleging that the deed conveyed defective title. The complaint alleges that a defect exists in the chain of title, which is the only contested issue. The conservator asks the attorney who prepared the real estate contract to defend the estate against the lawsuit. The attorney is the sole attesting witness to the deed's execution. The litigation lawyer will call the attorney to testify at the trial of the lawsuit only to prove the deed's execution.

Will it be proper for the attorney to represent the estate against the lawsuit?

A. No, because it is not necessary for the attorney to represent the estate in order to prevent substantial hardship to the estate.

B. No, because the attorney will be called as a witness in the lawsuit about execution of the deed.

C. Yes, because no contested issue exists regarding the deed's execution.

D. Yes, because the attorney lacks any beneficial interest pursuant to the deed.

QUESTION 54

An attorney is a sole practitioner. She represents a client in a case involving a few different types of law. When working on the case, the attorney discovers a complicated legal bankruptcy matter about which she lacks legal competence. Although she exercises due diligence in gaining some competence regarding the matter, the attorney reasonably believes that associating with a bankruptcy lawyer is necessary to ensure that she properly handles the matter. The attorney contacts and explains this situation to the client. She also explains that she wants to associate with another lawyer on this matter only. The client assents to the attorney' association with a bankruptcy lawyer she knows, who has competence concerning the matter.

Will it be proper for the attorney to associate with the bankruptcy lawyer?

A. Yes, because no regulations apply to the association.

B. Yes, because the client consented to the association after the attorney explained it to the client.

C. No, because the attorney personally knows the bankruptcy lawyer.

D. No, because the attorney cannot associate with the bankruptcy lawyer under these circumstances.

QUESTION #55

Three attorneys are members of the same bar. They all work in the same office building that has an outside sign stating "Law Offices." Each of them rent separate and adjacent office suites. They represent their own clients and do not share fees earned from this representation. Sometimes, they each refer prospective clients to one another without receiving any compensation for doing so. However, they equally pay for the costs of a secretary, paralegal, and answering service. They meet and decide to change the outside sign to read "Three Attorneys, Law Partners." That sign replaces the former one. The three attorneys have never entered into any type of formal partnership agreement or arrangement.

Are the three attorneys subject to discipline?

A.   No, because they equally share the costs of a secretary, paralegal, and answering service.

B.   No, because sometimes they refer prospective clients to each other.

C.   Yes, because the three attorneys have not entered into any type of partnership agreement or arrangement.

D.   Yes, because members of the bar can never refer to themselves as law partners.

QUESTION #56

A judge has a good reputation in the community surrounding the state court in which she serves. Her supporters respect her record as a jurist and trust her opinion on legal matters. The judge is friends with a couple who have a daughter. The daughter attends law school and wants to get a position clerking for a law firm when school is not in session. The daughter asks the judge for a letter of recommendation because she knows the judge and thinks that the letter could increase her prospects of working for a law firm. Wanting to help the daughter, the judge provides her with a general letter of recommendation addressed "to whom it may concern." Because the daughter has not worked for the judge, the letter simply refers to the daughter's character. The letter, which appears on court stationary, contains only truthful statements.

Will the judge will be subject to discipline?

A.   Yes, because she wrote the letter on court stationary.

B.   Yes, because she knows the daughter and is friends with her parents.

C.   No, because she knows the daughter.

D.   No, because the letter will afford the judge an improper advantage.

QUESTION #57

An attorney is a sole practitioner. Her general practice includes matters involving contract law, criminal law, domestic relations, property law, and torts. She does not handle legal matters involving wills, trusts, corporations, or partnerships. Late one Friday night, she receives a phone call while at her home. Her aunt informs her that her step-uncle suffered a near-fatal injury and was not expected to live much longer. Further, the aunt reveals that the step-uncle has no last will and testament. The aunt implores the attorney to meet with them as soon as possible in order to make a will for the step-uncle before he dies. The attorney replies that her law practice does not involve preparing wills, and she lacks the knowledge and skill to properly draft a will for the step-uncle. The aunt, however, insists that it is imperative that the attorney do this under the circumstances and would not accept "no" for an answer.

The attorney goes to the hospital and meets with the aunt and the step-uncle. His treating physician says that the step-uncle only has two days to live. The attorney takes detailed notes of the step-uncle's intentions about his property's disposition. The attorney tells the aunt and the step-uncle that on Saturday morning she will try to find a lawyer who specialized in wills who is available then to properly draft one. However, none of the lawyers in the phone book whose listing mentioned wills are in the office when she contacts them. Therefore, the attorney promptly drafts the step-uncle's will based on her notes and using a standard form. She delivers it to the step-uncle and has it duly executed.

Did the attorney engage in proper conduct?

A.   No, because the attorney lacked experience in or special training about wills.

B.   No, because the attorney lacked the legal competence to prepare the step-uncle's will.

C.   Yes, because in this emergency situation, it was impractical for the attorney to either refer the matter to, or associate with, another lawyer.

D.   Yes, because of the attorney's familial relationship with the aunt and the step-uncle.

QUESTION #58

A judge and her husband live in the same household. The judge is one of five trustees of a charitable trust for the local community's benefit. The husband serves as the trust's accountant. A corporation files a lawsuit against a company alleging tortious interference with a business relationship. The judge is scheduled to preside over the trial of the corporation's case against the company. Subsequently, the husband provides the trustees with a current accounting of the trust's assets. The total value of $1,000,000 includes 1 share of the company's stock, which has a current market value per share of $1. Although the judge then notices the trust's ownership of the company stock, she believes that it will not affect her handling of the corporation's case. The judge does not disqualify herself from presiding in the case.

Will the judge be subject to discipline?

A.   No, because the judge does not personally own shares of the company's stock.

B.   No, because the trust only possesses a *de minimis* economic interest in the company.

C.   Yes, because the judge cannot handle the case in a fair manner.

D.   Yes, because the results of the case will not impact the company's stock cost.

QUESTION #59

A landowner retains an attorney for the purpose of bringing a tort action against a neighbor. The attorney files the action alleging trespass and seeking injunctive relief to prevent future trespass by the neighbor upon the landowner's premises. A lawyer agrees to represent the neighbor. At the pre-trial conference in this action, the lawyer makes an offer of compromise. Acceptance of the offer would have two results. First, the neighbor would agree to stay off of the landowner's property and to pay liquidated damages to the landowner for any future instance of going on that property. Second, the attorney would be precluded from representing the landowner in any other type of legal matter involving the parties to the action. The attorney explains to the landowner that the effect of his accepting the offer of compromise would be to prevail in his action without going to trial, but that she could not represent him again in any other legal matter involving the neighbor. However, other lawyers could competently represent the landowner in such other legal matters. Moreover, the attorney considers the neighbor's offer of compromise to be in the landowner 's best interest, or the best way to accomplish her goals in this case.

Would it be proper for the attorney to recommend accepting the offer of compromise?

A.   No, because the offer would improperly prevent the attorney from representing the landowner in any other legal matter involving the neighbor.

B.   Yes, because other lawyers could provide the landowner with competent representation in any other legal matter involving the neighbor.

C.   Yes, because the attorney is only prevented from representing the landowner in any other legal matter involving the neighbor.

D.   Yes, because the attorney thinks that this is the best method for the landowner to achieve her objectives in this action, or is in her best interest.

QUESTION #60

Upon becoming members of the bar, two attorney who are friends, maintain separate law practices. In order to diversify and supplement their income, the two attorneys purchase an office building as co-tenants with two other non-lawyers. The non-lawyer co-tenants manage the building. No partnership exists between the attorneys and the two non-lawyers. The two attorneys maintain separate law offices in the building for five years until the one is elected as a trial court judge. The judge retains his co-tenancy in the building during his subsequent four-years on the bench.

Three other candidates are campaigning to unseat the judge at the end of his term of office. The judge tells the attorney co-tenant that he plans to appoint a new law clerk upon his reelection. The attorney co-tenant decides to financially support the judge as an incumbent judge seeking reelection. The attorney co-tenant contributes money to the judge's campaign in order to influence the judge to consider or appoint him as the new law clerk. After winning the election, the judge appoints the attorney co-tenant as his new law clerk.

Will the attorney co-tenant be subject to discipline for accepting the appointment by the lawyer?

A. No, because the attorney may accept the appointment under any circumstances.

B. No, because the attorney and judge have an established professional and financial relationship.

C. Yes, because they have an established professional and financial relationship.

D. Yes, because the attorney made the contribution for an improper purpose.

QUESTION #61

A state prosecutor files charges against a defendant alleging that she committed armed robbery. At the defendant's first court appearance in this case, the judge appoints an attorney as her defense counsel. The judge denies the attorney's request for bail.

After the first appearance, the prosecutor presents some plea agreement proposals to the attorney. Outside of the prosecutor's presence, the attorney discusses those proposals with the defendant. The defendant rejects them. The defendant insists upon pleading not guilty and demands a trial. The attorney then communicates the results of this discussion with the prosecutor adjacent to the defendant's holding cell. The attorney briefly steps away, leaving the prosecutor outside the defendant's cell. The defendant then asks the prosecutor if he would consider dropping the charges if the defendant turns state's evidence against someone else. Before walking away, the prosecutor tells the defendant that he cannot talk to him because the attorney represents him.

Will the prosecutor be subject to discipline?

A. Yes, because the prosecutor communicated with the defendant.

B. Yes, because the prosecutor presented the plea agreement proposals to the attorney, rather than the defendant.

C.   No, because the prosecutor declined to talk with the defendant.

D.   No, because the prosecutor has immunity.

QUESTION #62

A large insurance company serves its insureds in one state. The company's insurance policies protect the insureds' property. Recently, major storms and natural disasters have adversely affected the property of the state's population. In turn, the number and amount of their property insurance claims have reached a historically high level. Consequently, a committee of the state legislature is conducting hearings regarding the sufficiency and improvement of property insurance.

The company retains an attorney to perform most of its regulatory compliance work. The attorney has done this for the company for several years. The attorney handles at least half of all of the company's legal matters. The remainder is divided between in-house corporate counsel and a law firm that handles litigation.

Pursuant to the company's direction, the attorney testifies in the property insurance hearings of the state legislature's committee. The attorney's testimony reflected the position that the company wanted him to convey regarding property insurance. The appearance form that the attorney filed, however, did not refer to the company. Thus, the committee was not aware of the attorney's relationship with the company. The company paid the attorney for his time and expenses of giving that testimony.

Did the attorney engage in proper conduct?

A.   No, because the attorney did not reveal that he appeared as the company's retained counsel.

B.   No, because the company paid the attorney for testifying before the committee.

C.   Yes, because the attorney could not reveal his relationship with the company on account of the duty of client-lawyer confidentiality.

D.   Yes, because the attorney could not reveal his relationship with the company on account of the attorney-client evidentiary privilege.

QUESTION #63

An attorney, an associate in a law firm, practices business law. While at home one Saturday morning, a friend calls her. The friend exclaims that the police had just taken her only child, a young boy, into protective custody based on allegations of neglect and abuse. The friend swears that the boy only suffered injuries from another child and that the boy received appropriate medical treatment. The friend asks the attorney to help her regain custody of the boy immediately. The attorney replies "I have never practiced domestic relations law, but I will try to help." Finding no lawyer who specialized in protective child custody available on Saturday, the attorney goes to the police station. Her efforts on the friend's behalf do not secure the boy's release.

Was it proper for the attorney to assist the friend?

A.   No, because the attorney assisted the friend because of their relationship.

B.   No, because the attorney lacked the requisite legal competence to handle the friend's matter.

C.   Yes, because the attorney attempted to obtain the boy's release from the police station.

D.   Yes, because the attorney tried to represent the friend in a way that was reasonably necessary in that situation.

QUESTION #64

In January, a plaintiff retains a litigation attorney in order to bring a defamation lawsuit against a defendant, whom a defense lawyer represents. In April, a judge appoints the litigation attorney as defense counsel for an accused in a felony criminal case. A prosecutor advises the litigation attorney that the prosecutor will be ready for trial in July. The plaintiff notifies the litigation attorney that she could participate in her civil trial throughout the summer. At a civil pretrial conference, the litigation attorney, the defense lawyer, and the judge schedule the plaintiff's trial for August. The plaintiff does not attend the conference. The litigation attorney does not ask for the plaintiff's approval of the trial date after the conference. However, the litigation attorney seasonably notifies the plaintiff of the trial date, and accurately advises that it would not adversely impact her interests. At a criminal pretrial conference, the litigation attorney, the prosecutor, and the judge set the accused's trial for July. No local criminal court rule regarding speedy trials applies.

Did the litigation attorney act properly by setting a civil trial date without the plaintiff's approval?

A.   No, because the attorney is allowed to control the scheduling of trials in order to expedite litigation.

B.   Yes, because no local criminal court rule regarding speedy trials applied.

C.   Yes, because the date set for the civil trial does not prejudice the plaintiff's interests.

D.   Yes, because criminal trial scheduling usually has priority over civil trial scheduling.

QUESTION #65

An inventor retains an attorney to assist with licensing his patented invention. The inventor accurately describes the invention, an electric vehicle battery, to the attorney as capable of powering an electric vehicle further and faster -- but not longer before recharge -- than other comparable batteries. On the inventor's behalf, the attorney contacts another lawyer, who represents a manufacturer, about licensing and producing the invention. The attorney describes the invention as capable of powering an electric vehicle the "furthest, fastest, and longest before recharge of any battery ever produced."

Will the attorney be subject to discipline?

A.   No, because the attorney made his statement to the lawyer instead of the manufacturer.

B.   No, because the attorney's description of the invention constituted "puffing" for sales purposes, rather than a false statement.

C.   Yes, because the attorney made a misrepresentation of material fact to the lawyer.

D.   Yes, because the attorney overstated the invention's capabilities.

QUESTION #66

A defendant, a foreign citizen, lives and works in the United States. Due to his naivety, the defendant becomes socially involved with unsavory characters. In his dealings with them, a personal disagreement becomes heated and one of them runs at the defendant with his clenched fists raised. At the last possible moment, the defendant steps aside to avoid the attacker. The attacker rushes by the defendant and crashes through a 10-story window, plummeting to his death. The other witnesses to this incident are the attacker's friends. In order to avenge his death, they all agree to the same story that the defendant intentionally threw the attacker out the window.

The witnesses tell their story to the police. The police arrest the defendant. The defendant makes a written statement describing his recollection of the events. A prosecutor files murder charges against the defendant. The court appoints an attorney as defense counsel for the defendant. The court releases the defendant into the attorney's custody subject to the requirement that he not leave the metropolitan area. The attorney believes the defendant's version of events, but she cannot prove them without any corroborating witness testimony. The attorney believes that the only way that the defendant will receive justice is if his case does not go to trial. The attorney tells the defendant that if he returns to his country he cannot be tried for the offense because the United States does not have an extradition treaty with that country. The defendant returns to his country.

Will the attorney be subject to discipline?

A.   No, because the defendant gave a written statement indicating his innocence.

B.   No, because the attorney believed the defendant's version of events.

C.   Yes, because the attorney's counsel caused the defendant to flee the court's jurisdiction and United State's extradition power in order to avoid prosecution.

D.   Yes, because the defendant violated the conditions of his release.

QUESTION #67

A plaintiff corporation brings an antitrust action against a defendant corporation in federal court. The court assigns the case to a judge. The case raises several issues of first impression arising under recently enacted federal antitrust law. After the parties complete discovery, the judge disposes of several pretrial motions and conducts a pre-trial conference. Once the judge is ready for trial based on her familiarity with the law and facts, she discovers that her husband, a stockbroker, owns a significant quantity of the defendant corporation's stock.

The judge concludes that this case's outcome could substantially affect her husband's financial interest in the defendant corporation. While the judge thinks that she would fairly adjudicate the case, she discloses the husband's interest to the parties and their counsel. After she asks them to waive disqualification, they agree to do so with her participation.

Will it be proper for the judge to preside over the case?

A.   No, because the parties cannot waive the judge's disqualification that is mandatory due to the husband's economic interest.

B.   No, because the parties have not effectively waived the judge's disqualification under the circumstances.

C.   Yes, because the judge is especially prepared to be this case's presiding judge.

D.   Yes, because the judge believes that she can be impartial despite the husband's ownership of the large corporation stock.

QUESTION #68

An attorney runs a commercial for his law practice on several local radio stations. The broadcast range of the stations is limited to the jurisdiction in which he is licensed to practice law. The entire commercial consists of the attorney's own recorded voice saying:

"If you need effective legal representation, please call me. The toll-free number for a no obligation initial consultation is 888-888-8888."

The attorney maintains a file containing the commercial's script, his recording of it, and all information from the radio stations regarding when the commercial will be run and its cost.

Is the attorney's commercial proper?

A. Yes, because the commercial complies with a.   .⌐quirements.

B. No, because he did not pay a professional to record the commercial.

C. No, because the commercial does not indicate whether a fee applies to the initial consultation.

D. No, because the attorney did not identify himself or his office location in the commercial.

QUESTION #69

A plaintiff retains an attorney. The attorney represents the plaintiff in civil litigation against a defendant. The plaintiff prevails and receives an award of damages pursuant to the judgment. The plaintiff's retainer fee fully compensates the attorney. No balance remains for repayment to the plaintiff. The defendant sends the attorney a check for $75,000, the entire amount of damages awarded. The attorney endorses the check, which was payable to the attorney, to the plaintiff and mails it to the plaintiff. The plaintiff deposits the check without objection.

Will the attorney be subject to discipline?

A. No, because the plaintiff received the proper amount of damages.

B. No, because the plaintiff did not object to the check.

C. Yes, because the attorney improperly processed the check.

D. Yes, because the attorney failed to pay the plaintiff in cash.

QUESTION #70

An attorney opens her own law office after becoming a bar member. The attorney registers with a trial court to be appointed as defense counsel. A prosecutor charges a defendant with unrelated felony and misdemeanor offenses. A judge of the trial court appoints the attorney to represent the defendant. The defendant demands a trial by jury on all charges. The attorney obtains all relevant information from the defendant and performs research for trial purposes. After spending several days working on the case, she realizes that her legal skill and understanding are insufficient to provide effective counsel to the defendant. The attorney tells the defendant what she realized. The attorney gets the defendant's informed consent to her continued sole representation.

Will the attorney's representation of the defendant be proper?

A. Yes, because the trial judge appointed her as sole counsel.

B. Yes, because the defendant knowingly and voluntarily accepted her continued representation.

C. No, because the attorney lacks appropriate legal skill and understanding.

D. No, because the attorney is not a certified specialist in criminal defense.

QUESTION #71

An attorney represents a plaintiff in a breach of contract action against a defendant. The attorney secures a judgment in favor of the plaintiff. The defendant mails a check to the attorney for $15,000, the amount of damages set forth in the judgment. The attorney places the check in the attorney's client trust account. The plaintiff has previously fully paid the attorney's fees and costs of representation in the contract action.

Upon learning of the plaintiff's judgment, a creditor contacts the attorney regarding the plaintiff's past due debt. The creditor asserts that the plaintiff owes $2,400 for missing six vehicle loan payments. The creditor claims that it is entitled to a payment of that sum out of the amount of damages that the plaintiff recovered. The creditor warns the attorney that it has a lien on the damages and that it would assert its legal rights, including repossession of the vehicle, if the demanded payment of $2,400 is not made immediately. The attorney promptly communicates this information to the plaintiff, who replies:

"It does not matter what the creditor says. That vehicle is my second car, so I do not really need it. The creditor can do what it wants to. They can have that worthless piece of junk back. I have bad credit already, so whatever happens cannot make my credit any worse. Just mail me a check for $15,000."

Applicable law provides that the creditor has a lawful claim, which the attorney has a legal duty to protect, and that the claim is not frivolous.

Will the attorney be subject to discipline for doing what the plaintiff requested?

A. No, because the plaintiff was entitled to the damages recovered.

B. No, because the creditor was not entitled to the damages recovered.

C. Yes, because the client and the creditor both claim interests in the damages recovered.

D. Yes, because the attorney informed the plaintiff that the creditor would enforce its legal rights against the plaintiff.

QUESTION #72

A developer pre-sells 100 homes in a subdivision before constructing them. The standard form purchase contract states that each home will be identical to a model home's design. However, 75 of the homes are built using a different design having one less bathroom. An attorney files a breach of contract action against the developer on behalf of the 75 homeowners. The developer makes an offer of compromise providing an aggregate settlement of all of the homeowners' claims in the amount of $750,000. Based on research and consultation, the attorney determines the approximate value of each of the homeowners' claims, which constitutes their respective settlement amount. This amount is based on the estimated market value of the missing bathroom, subject to adjustment based on when the home was built.

The attorney considers this to be a reasonable and equitable method for dividing the damages among all of the homeowners. The developer makes its offer contingent upon acceptance by each and every one of the homeowners of each homeowner's settlement amount. The attorney advises each of the homeowners of the offer's total amount and the homeowner's individual settlement amount. All of the homeowners are willing to accept the offer based on the settlement amount. But the attorney has not revealed to any of the homeowners the respective value of every other one of the homeowners' settlement amount. The attorney is concerned that doing this could possibly undermine the prospects of the offer's universal acceptance if some of the homeowners believe that their settlement amount is not fair in comparison to the settlement amount of any of the other homeowners.

Will the attorney be subject to discipline if the offer is accepted without further disclosure?

A. No, because revealing all settlement amounts could undermine the prospects of the offer's universal acceptance.

B. No, because each of the homeowners will receive a fair settlement amount and they each will accept it.

C. Yes, because the attorney is assisting the developer in making an aggregate settlement of all of the homeowners' claims.

D. Yes, because none of the homeowner need to know the settlement amount that any of the other homeowners will receive.

QUESTION #73

An attorney represents a plaintiff in a tort action against a defendant company. The company sells widgets. The plaintiff's complaint makes a defective product claim seeking recovery of damages. The complaint alleges that plaintiff sustained personal injuries while using the widget as the company intended. Specifically, the complaint asserts that the company's defective design of the widget caused the plaintiff's injuries. During pre-trial discovery, the attorney makes a proper request for documents from the company about the product's design. In reviewing the documents requested, the company's in-house lawyer finds a widget designer's handwritten note stating that, due to the widget's design, the widget could cause the type of injury that plaintiff sustained. The in-house lawyer does not provide the note or refer to it in response to the request for documents or otherwise.

Will the in-house lawyer be subject to discipline?

A. No, because the note is confidential.

B. No, because the note is work product.

C. Yes, because he has a constitutional duty to disclose the note.

D. Yes, because he prevented the plaintiff from obtaining the note.

QUESTION #74

An attorney works as corporate counsel for a health maintenance organization. The attorney reviews applications for payment of medical care by the organization. The attorney provides legal advice regarding how to handle the applications. A patient applies for medical care. The attorney reviews the patient's application before leaving the organization to work in a law firm.

Pursuant to the attorney's advice, the organization denies the patient's application. A few months later, the patient goes to the attorney's office. The patient requests that the attorney accept him as a client in his proposed lawsuit against the organization to recover payment for his medical care.

Will it be proper for the attorney to accept the patient as a client?

A. Yes, because of the attorney's knowledge and experience.

B. Yes, because the attorney does not represent the organization.

C. No, because the attorney represented the organization.

D. No, because the attorney has not worked at the law firm long enough.

QUESTION #75

A watercraft insurance company employs an attorney in its legal department. The attorney examines claims made by the company's insureds for maritime losses. The attorney gives legal counsel to the company about whether to pay the claims. An insured individual makes a claim for loss of her yacht, which a hurricane destroyed. After the attorney examines the individual's claim, the company fully pays for her loss. Instead of replacing the yacht, the individual buys a kayak, which insurance does not cover.

The attorney leaves the company and opens his own law office as a general practitioner. Some years later, the company's promotional motorboat collides with the individual's kayak, causing her personal injuries. The individual goes to the attorney's office seeking representation in her potential tort lawsuit against the company.

Will it be proper for the attorney to represent her?

A.   Yes, because of the subject matter of the representation.

B.   Yes, because the attorney does not represent the company.

C.   No, because the attorney represented the company.

D.   No, because the attorney examined the individual's claim.

QUESTION #76

An attorney represents a plaintiff in a civil dispute against a defendant. To formalize the arrangement for representation, the attorney provides a standard retainer contract and a waiver form, which he typically uses with most clients. The contract includes the following terms:

The client will provide an initial retainer fee of $ _____. After this amount has been applied to legal fees earned in representing the client, the client will timely pay all of the attorney's other bills for legal fees. The attorney's hourly rate is $150.00. By signing this contract and a waiver form, the client waives any and all legal malpractice claims that the client has or acquires as a result of the attorney's representation.

A waiver form is attached to the contract. The attorney advises the client that she should have another lawyer review the retainer contract and waiver form before she signs them. The client, however, decides not to do obtain the advice of another lawyer. Although the client has no other lawyer represent her when entering into the agreement, she duly signs the retainer contract and waiver. The attorney charges a reasonable hourly rate and that is qualified to represent the client.

Are the lawyer's retainer contract and waiver form proper?

A.   No, because they seek to prospectively limit the attorney's exposure to legal malpractice liability.

B.   No, because the attorney uses the same forms with most clients.

C.   Yes, because the attorney provided consideration by agreeing to represent the client.

D.   Yes, because the attorney's hourly rate is reasonable and he is qualified to represent the client.

QUESTION #77

An attorney and a licensed securities dealer, execute a contract. The contract provides that the attorney will only refer to the dealer any of her clients who want to trade stocks or obtain related investment services. The contract also provides that the dealer will refer any of his customers that need legal representation only to the attorney in exchange for a small payment. The attorney mainly practices securities law. The attorney does not tell her clients about the contract. The attorney and the dealer charge their clients reasonable fees for their respective professional services. With the exception of the small payment for a referral made to the dealer, neither of them share in each others' fees paid by their clients and customers.

Will the attorney be subject to discipline based on this contract?

A. No, because the dealer does not share in the attorney's fees and the attorney does not share in the dealer's fees.

B. No, because neither the dealer nor the attorney charge unreasonable fees for their respective professional services.

C. Yes, because the attorney is paying the dealer for referrals.

D. Yes, because under this contract the attorney is essentially practicing law with the dealer, a non-lawyer.

QUESTION #78

A husband and wife are experiencing serious marital difficulties. The wife retains an attorney, who files a divorce action on behalf of the wife. Another lawyer agrees to represent the husband in the action. The extent of the parties' irreconcilable differences has caused them to become very adversarial. Moreover, the wife engaged in an extramarital affair. Feeling particularly vindictive, the husband tells his lawyer that he wants him to take an aggressive approach to litigation. The husband says: "My wife does not deserve any favors or concessions from us. We need to win this case even if it's on procedural grounds."

The husband's lawyer serves the wife's attorney with a notice of taking the wife's deposition. The wife's attorney writes the husband's lawyer with a request that he reschedule the deposition because it is set for the same date as the wife's surgery for a life-threatening condition. The husband objects to rescheduling the deposition.

Will the husband's lawyer be subject to discipline if he agrees to reschedule the deposition?

A. No, because the husband's rights would not be prejudiced by rescheduling the deposition.

B. No, because the husband has the right to determine the means and objectives of legal representation.

C. Yes, because the lawyer would not be following the husband's directive.

D. Yes, because the lawyer lacked the husband's approval to reschedule the deposition.

QUESTION #79

A client retains an attorney to represent her in estate planning matters. The client and the attorney enter into a valid retainer agreement, pursuant to which she issues a check to the attorney in the requested amount of $2,000. The attorney deposits the check in a trust account for the client. The agreement requires the client to issue another $2,000 check to the attorney upon receipt of notice from the attorney that the account balance is $100 or less. The bank that holds the account imposes a monthly service charge on all accounts for which the balance falls below $100. After the attorney completes half of the estate planning work for the client, he properly draws his earned fee against the client's trust account. At that point, its balance falls to zero and the attorney mails the client notice of that fact. However, the client does not receive that notice because it arrives the day that the police declare her a missing person. The attorney learns of the declaration in the local news. Then the bank provides the attorney with notice that it will impose a $10 service charge on the client's trust account because it has a zero balance. The attorney withdraws $10 from his general account and deposits $10 into the client's trust account.

Will the attorney be subject to discipline for commingling funds?

A.   Yes, because the attorney made an improper deposit.

B.   Yes, because the attorney mixed his funds with the client's funds.

C.   No, because the attorney made a proper deposit.

D.   No, because of the client's legal status.

QUESTION #80

An attorney is a sole practitioner in a small town. The nature of his law practice and scope of experience requires a support staff of one secretary and three paralegals. The staff all report to the attorney as their supervisor, who delegates secretarial, clerical, and paralegal work to them. For purposes of performing their work, the staff may access the files of the attorney's clients. The attorney compensates his staff with both hourly wages and a profit sharing arrangement. The profit sharing occurs every six months. The staff shares in five percent of the attorney's legal fees.

Is it proper for the attorney to pay the staff in this manner?

A.   No, because an attorney may not share legal fees with non-lawyers.

B.   No, because the attorney is assisting the staff as non-lawyers in practicing law.

C.   No, because the staff have access to his clients' files.

D.   Yes, because the staff lacks control over the attorney's professional judgment.

QUESTION #81

A girl goes to the police and reports that her dance instructor inappropriately touched her during a private dance lesson at his dance studio. The police investigate the matter and find no other evidence that corroborates the girl's accusation. The police cannot question the instructor in person because he is out of the country. The police present this information to a prosecutor, a lawyer, who is assigned to the case's investigation and prosecution. Seeking publicity to support his reelection campaign, the prosecutor holds a press conference. At the conference, the prosecutor describes the girl's accusation in detail, which the media broadcasts in full. The prosecutor promises to hold the instructor accountable. The media conduct a survey that produces results showing that a vast majority of people believe that the instructor is guilty of a crime. Upon the instructor's return to the country, he retains a defense attorney. With the instructor's permission, the defense attorney calls and holds a press conference. The defense attorney truthfully states that the instructor has never met or taught the girl, who later admits that she falsely accused the instructor.

Will the defense attorney be subject to discipline for holding the press conference?

A.   Yes, because he called and participated in the press conference.

B.   Yes, because he made a statement about what his client, the instructor, told him.

C.   No, because he made a statement in order to protect the instructor.

D.   No, because the instructor gave him permission to have the press conference.

QUESTION #82

An attorney works for a state's law enforcement department after becoming a member of the bar. While serving in that position, the attorney directly participates in several prosecutions against parties who perpetrated criminal offenses against the public interest. These offenses did not affect the attorney's personal economic interests. Following the attorney's election to the state's court of appeals, the attorney resigns his position with the department. Some of the prosecutions with which he was involved are pending as cases on the state court of appeals' docket. Upon becoming a judge on the court, the court clerk assigns one of those cases to him. The judge believes that he can make an impartial decision about the case, but does not disclose his role in the case.

Would it be proper for the judge to decide the case?

A.   No, because the judge failed to disclose his role in the case.

B.   No, because the judge worked for the department when the case was prosecuted.

C.   No, because the judge directly participated in the department's prosecution of the case.

D.   Yes, because the judge lacks any personal economic interest the criminal case.

QUESTION #83

A judge serves on the bench in a federal district court. For several years, the judge has been an uncompensated member of the state bar's board of a philanthropy. Every year the board of philanthropy hosts a fundraising dinner at which a person who is considered worthy of recognition for serving their community is honored. At this year's dinner, the state bar plans to recognize the judge for 20 years of public service.

The state bar's "public testimonial committee" has announced that it will accept special contributions from both lawyers and non-lawyers. The committee will apply these contributions towards paying for a sculpture bust of the judge, which the committee will give to the judge. The committee decides to take these steps after determining that they were lawful and ethical for the state bar, the committee, the philanthropy, contributing lawyers and non-lawyers, and the judge. The committee takes those steps and gives the bust to the judge at the dinner. After receiving the bust, the judge does not submit any regulatory paperwork that refers to it.

Will the judge be subject to discipline?

A.   Yes, because the judge accepted the sculpted bust as a gift.

B.   Yes, because the judge did not officially account for receiving the sculpted bust.

C.   Yes, because the judge received the sculpted bust incident to the public testimonial.

D.   No, because the judge has not been compensated for serving on the philanthropy's board.

QUESTION #84

A law firm primarily practices insurance defense. After enjoying several years of success, the firm falls on hard times. One of the firm's partners is a neighbor of a world-renowned insurance defense attorney. The world-renowned insurance defense attorney has a substantial roster of clients and is well-connected in the insurance industry. The firm partners believe that the new business generated by the addition of the world-renowned insurance defense attorney would breathe new life into the firm. The firm's attorneys unanimously agree to recruit the world-renowned insurance defense attorney as a new partner. The world-renowned insurance defense attorney agrees to the arrangement and becomes a new partner. The firm enters into an agreement with the new partner. The agreement obligates the firm to pay the new partner 10% of total profits each year. The firm is obligated to continue to make payments to the estate of the new partner for 100 years after the new partner's death.

Will the firm be subject to discipline for this agreement?

A.   No, because the agreement is lawful and ethical.

B.   No, because an attorney can enter into any agreement with the firm.

C.   Yes, because the agreement is unlawful.

D.   Yes, because the agreement is unreasonable.

QUESTION #85

A hunter lawfully hunts deer on state land. While there, the hunter receives a gunshot wound from an unidentifiable shooter. The state land is located near the defendant landowner's private property. A prosecutor charges the defendant with a felony for allegedly shooting the hunter. The defendant retains an attorney to defend him. The attorney calls and speaks by phone with the defendant's only potential witness. The witness says that on the day of the shooting, she was with the defendant in the state. The attorney finds no evidence contradicting what the witness said. At trial, the attorney does not present any evidence that the defendant was absent from the state when the shooting occurred. However, in closing argument, the attorney states that the defendant was out of the state when the shooting occurred.

Will the attorney be subject to discipline?

A.   Yes, because the attorney did not present any evidence to support the statement.

B.   Yes, because the attorney said that the defendant was out of the state at the time of the shooting.

C.   No, because the attorney has a duty to zealously defend every client.

D.   No, because the attorney used best efforts in representing the client.

QUESTION #86

The police arrest a defendant based on probable cause that she is involved in a reported kidnapping of a victim. The kidnappers demand that the state pay a ransom, which the state refuses to pay.   At the defendant's request, an attorney represents her during custodial interrogation by the police. The defendant does not make any incriminating statements to the police. Afterwards, the defendant informs the attorney in confidence of the kidnapping victim's location. The defendant tells the attorney that the defendant's accomplice will kill the victim if the state does not pay the ransom as demanded. The attorney knows that the state will not pay the ransom. The attorney thinks that the defendant is telling the truth because he has previously defended her in other criminal matters.

Will it be proper for the attorney to reveal the defendant's statement to the police?

A.   No, because the defendant's statement is subject to and protected by client-lawyer confidentiality.

B. No, because doing so would be in conflict with the defendant's best interest.

C. Yes, because the defendant's admission of guilt to the attorney is not protected by client-lawyer confidentiality.

D. Yes, because the defendant's statement is not protected by client-lawyer confidentiality because of the type of information it provides.

QUESTION #87

For several years, a small city employs an attorney on a part-time basis to handle its litigation. When not working for the city, the attorney represents clients as a sole practitioner. The local rules authorize this arrangement.

The attorney represents the city in a civil action against a citizen to recover unpaid property taxes. The city recovers a judgment against the citizen that has yet to be enforced. The citizen approaches the attorney and requests that the attorney represent the citizen in litigation against the city. The attorney's political beliefs align with the citizen's position, so the attorney agrees to represent the citizen in a lawsuit challenging the validity of the city's property tax ordinances and enforcement procedures. Before accepting the representation, the attorney formally ceases representing the city. The attorney does not request that the city consent to her representation of the citizen in this case.

Will the attorney be subject to discipline for agreeing to take the citizen's case?

A. No, because the attorney ceased representing the city before representing the citizen.

B. No, because the attorney can have clients while being employed by the city.

C. Yes, because the attorney failed to obtain the city's oral consent to representing the citizen.

D. Yes, because the attorney substantially participated in the city's civil action against the citizen.

QUESTION #88

A law firm handles civil litigation. The firm agrees to represent a client in a medical malpractice action arising from outpatient care of the client. The firm's managing partner directed an associate attorney, who recently became a member of the bar, to prosecute the client's civil action. The associate attorney's research did not discover a special service of process provision for medical malpractice actions. Consequently, the associate attorney improperly served process, which resulted in the dismissal of the client's action with prejudice. This precluded the client from recovering on her claim worth $3,000. Both the firm and the associate attorney may have civil liability exposure in the client's potential legal malpractice action.

Will the associate attorney be subject to discipline?

A.   Yes, because the associate attorney had a duty to decline undertaking responsibility for the case.

B.   Yes, because the associate attorney did not fulfill her duties when acting at another attorney's direction.

C.   No, because the associate attorney acted at the managing attorney's direction.

D.   No, because of the action's minimal dollar value qualifies as *de minimis*.

QUESTION #89

An attorney serves as a sales company's corporate counsel. The sales company employs a large number of people, including a sales person. In January, the sales company makes an unsecured loan to the sales person of $500 for which she signs an enforceable agreement to repay the sales company. In May, the sales person resigns from the sales company. At that time, however, the sales person has not made any payment to the sales company of the balance due on the loan. The attorney does not learn of the sales person's resignation until December, when the sales company's accountant notices that the $500 debt remains unpaid. The accountant calls and speaks with the sales person about making payment arrangements to satisfy this debt. She replies that if the sales company "wants me to pay, it will have to make me pay." The accountant then explains the situation to the attorney. The attorney's research determines that the statute of limitations on the loan has not expired and that the agreement could be enforced in small claims court. He tells the sales company's president: "The sales company has a valid agreement with the sales person. It is enforceable by means of a small claims action, which I could file before the statute of limitations expires. The sales company could prevail in this action. However, the time and effort involved in pursuing this claim, which could involve my appearance in court with the accountant, might be more than it is worth. Also, enforcing this agreement might harm the sales company's business interests if the sales person were to tell others about it. How will her former co-workers here and/or our clients whose accounts she used to serve, think about the sales company? I recommend that the sales company does not enforce this agreement with the sales person."

The president decides not to enforce the loan agreement.

Was the attorney's conduct proper?

A.   No, because the attorney's advice included both legal and economic factors.

B.   No, because the attorney's advice not to pursue the small claim violated his duty of zealous advocacy.

C.   Yes, because the president accepted the attorney's advice and decided against enforcing the loan agreement.

D.   Yes, because the attorney's advice could include both legal and economic factors.

QUESTION #90

A prosecutor represents the state in a criminal trial. An attorney serves as defense counsel. The trial judge renders a judgment finding the defendant guilty of vehicular homicide. Pursuant to the defendant's informed consent, the attorney appeals the judgment of conviction. The attorney drafts the appellate brief after checking the evidence and trial testimony. In the brief, the attorney writes that: "Undisputed evidence shows that the traffic light was green for the defendant when her vehicle approached it and passed under it as the deceased victim ran in front of her oncoming vehicle." However, one of the prosecutor's witnesses testified at trial that the traffic light was red for the defendant when her vehicle struck the deceased victim who was walking across the street. The attorney has both previously heard and read this testimony.

The attorney experiences a severe stroke a few days before oral arguments before the state court of appeals are scheduled. The attorney's secretary contacts a new lawyer, who is "of counsel" to the attorney's law practice. The new lawyer decides to stand in the attorney's place at oral arguments. Although the attorney cannot communicate with the new lawyer, his secretary provides him with the appellate brief and the trial transcript. Due to time constraints, the new lawyer only reads the brief and some of the transcript, but does not read the contradictory testimony of the prosecutor's witness. Presuming that the attorney's entire brief is accurate, the new lawyer's oral argument quotes its statement that undisputed evidence shows that the traffic light was green for the defendant when her vehicle drove under it and the deceased victim ran out in front of the vehicle.

Will the new lawyer be subject to discipline for quoting from the brief?

A.   No, because the new lawyer was unaware of the quoted excerpt's falsity.

B.   No, because the new lawyer did not make the first instance of misrepresentation.

C.   Yes, because the quoted text involved a false statement.

D.   Yes, because the new lawyer did not diligently research whether the quoted text was true or false.

QUESTION #91

An criminal law attorney and a probate lawyer are members of the bar in the same state. The state bar provides an assistance program for lawyers suffering from addictions. The criminal law attorney practices as a sole practitioner and serves on a state bar committee that oversees the assistance program. The probate lawyer works for a law firm and primarily handles matters involving wills, estates, and trusts. The probate lawyer serves as the trustee of several trusts containing substantial assets of high-value clients. The probate lawyer goes to the criminal law attorney and retains him because he is concerned about having some criminal liability. The probate lawyer tells the criminal law attorney that one time he took some of his client's funds and used them to support his gambling addiction. The criminal law attorney advises him not to do that again and to use the lawyer assistance program's services.

Is the criminal law attorney obligated to report the probate lawyer's misuse of clients' trust funds to the state's professional authority?

A. No, because the criminal law attorney obtained this information while representing the probate lawyer.

B. No, because a lawyer in the probate lawyer's law firm having knowledge of the lawyer's misconduct is obligated to report it.

C. Yes, because the criminal law attorney obtained this information while representing the lawyer.

D. Yes, because the criminal law attorney's failure to report the probate lawyer's conduct would help conceal the probate lawyer's breach of fiduciary duty.

QUESTION #92

A plaintiff and a defendant are litigating a complex commercial law case before a judge. The case involves some novel issues of Uniform Commercial Code (UCC) law pertaining to interstate secured transactions. An attorney, who specializes in UCC law and does not represent either party to the case, makes a telephone call to the judge. The attorney and the judge extensively discuss the case and the governing law. The judge makes detailed notes on her conversation with the attorney and keeps them with her other materials regarding the case. The judge does not then disclose the phone call or the contents of her notes to either the plaintiff or the defendant.

After the parties finish presenting their respective cases, the judge takes the case under advisement as the trier of fact and law. Along with the parties' pleadings, the judge takes the notes of the attorney's phone call and its points into consideration when preparing her written opinion.

Was it proper for the judge to utilize her notes based on the attorney's phone call?

A. No, because the judge did not disclose the attorney's call and her notes to the parties.

B. No, because the judge cannot obtain the opinion of a disinterested third-party expert.

C. Yes, because the attorney called the judge and the judge did not call the attorney.

D. Yes, because no client with interests that this case's outcome could affect was represented by the attorney.

QUESTION #93

A plaintiff's attorney agrees to represent a plaintiff in a tort action alleging claims of products liability in negligence and strict liability. The action alleges that a defective vehicle manufactured by the defendant corporation's caused the plaintiff's severe and permanent injuries when its gas tank spontaneously exploded. A defense lawyer represents the defendant, which agrees with him to make an offer of compromise.

The offer is for a $1,000,000 lump sum payment in exchange for dismissal of the tort action with prejudice. The plaintiff's attorney describes the offer to the plaintiff and tells him that he probably could obtain more damages by means of a jury trial than by the compromise. The plaintiff decides to accept the recommendation that he reject the offer. The plaintiff's attorney communicates that rejection to the defense lawyer. In response, the defense lawyer sends a letter directly to the plaintiff asking him to compromise because the defense lawyer reasonably believes that the plaintiff's attorney wants a trial to get free media coverage.

Will the defense lawyer be subject to discipline?

A. No, if the lawyer based his request upon a reasonable belief.

B. No, because the plaintiff's attorney based her recommendation on an improper motive.

C. Yes, because the plaintiff was represented by an attorney.

D. Yes, because the plaintiff decided not to compromise.

QUESTION #94

A prosecutor charges a defendant with murder, a capital crime. The prosecutor alleges that the defendant's speeding vehicle struck and killed a victim in front of eyewitnesses. This fatal collision occurred on a clear and sunny day when victim had the right of way in a crosswalk. The defendant retains a high-profile attorney to represent him. The attorney is widely known for representing criminal clients in publicized trials. The prosecutor offers to reduce the charge to involuntary manslaughter, a non-capital crime, if the defendant agrees to plead guilty to the charge. The attorney recommends that the defendant reject the offer because a jury possibly could acquit the defendant of the murder charge. Consequently, the defendant rejects the offer. Later, the prosecutor hears the attorney tell a friend that he recommended that the defendant reject the offer because he wants to go to trial due to its media coverage. The attorney provides effective assistance of counsel at the trial, which has media coverage. The defendant is convicted of murder and sentenced to death.

Based on the law and facts, the prosecutor reasonably believes that the attorney placed his personal desire for media coverage over the defendant's best interest in not going to trial in this case.

Will it be proper for the prosecutor to inform the relevant professional authority of his concerns about the attorney's motive for recommending rejection of the offer?

A.   No, because the attorney provided the defendant with effective assistance of counsel at trial.

B.   No, because the defendant could have been acquitted as a result of a trial, which could not have resulted from accepting the offer.

C.   Yes, because the prosecutor has evidence that the defendant's rejection of the offer is attributable to the attorney's desire for media coverage.

D.   Yes, because the trial of the case received extensive media coverage.

QUESTION #95

An attorney employs several paralegals as assistants in his law practice. These paralegals have credentials from properly accredited academic institutions. The attorney represents a client. One of the paralegals fails to make an entry in her case calendar for the critical filing deadline for the client's civil cause of action. Consequently, a filing required to prosecute the client's action does not timely occur. As a result, the client's action can neither be maintained nor reinstated.

Which of the following statements accurately describes the attorney's professional culpability?

A.   The attorney is NOT subject to discipline unless the attorney negligently supervised the paralegal, but the attorney is subject to civil liability.

B.   The attorney is NOT subject to either discipline or civil liability if the attorney was not personally negligent.

C.   On the basis of vicarious liability, the attorney is subject to both discipline and civil liability.

D.   The client may decide if the attorney is either subject to discipline or civil liability.

QUESTION #96

A physician, a medical doctor, would like to formalize a professional relationship with an attorney. The attorney's practice exclusively involves medical malpractice actions. The attorney believes that this relationship would benefit her practice because the physician is a medical malpractice expert who regularly provides testimony in these types of cases. The physician would like to be the attorney 's partner, and make this arrangement evident in advertisements of their firm, as well as on its letterhead and in as listed in phone books, etc. These materials would identify the professional titles and degrees of both the physician and the attorney.

Will the attorney be subject to discipline for entering into this proposed relationship?

A.   No, because it will provide clients with the benefit of the physician's and the attorney 's combined experience and expertise.

B.   No, if only the attorney will provide legal advice to clients.

C.   Yes, because a partnership of the attorney and the physician would involve rendering legal services to clients.

D.   Yes, because the attorney would receive other non-legal fees in addition to legal fees.

QUESTION #97

Two accountants, a brother and sister, decide to form an accounting partnership. They retain an attorney who assists them by preparing and filing the requisite documents. The two partners equally share profits, losses, and control of their partnership.

A year after forming the partnership, a client brings an action against the partners and the partnership. The attorney agrees to represent the partnership and both of the partners individually in a civil action that a client brought against them. The attorney provides this representation in compliance with all applicable law and ethical rules. However, during this representation, the sister fails to inform the brother of certain partnership information that would have supported their objectives of representation. The partners and partnership lost the case after a trial.

Subsequently, the brother requests that the attorney file a tort lawsuit against the sister on the basis of the sister's negligence in failing to provide the missing partnership information in the prior, proper representation. The brother reasonably believes that if his sister had provided this information, the results of litigation would have been different.

Will it be proper for the attorney to litigate the brother's tort lawsuit?

A.   No, because the attorney represented both the brother and sister in the civil action in which the sister allegedly negligently failed to provide information to her brother.

B.   No, because a different lawyer will represent the sister in the brother's lawsuit.

C.   Yes, because the attorney did not receive the information during the clients' joint civil action.

D.   Yes, if the brother reasonably believed that if the sister had provided the information, the results of litigation would have been different.

QUESTION #98

Two family law attorneys separately practice law in a jurisdiction. The attorneys decide to form a partnership and both move into a new office together. To announce their partnership and obtain new clients, they run a radio commercial in the jurisdiction. A professional announcer provides the name of the law firm, the names of the attorneys, and the firm's office address. The announcer continues to state:

"The attorneys have combined forces to provide you with effective and competent representation. The attorneys want to put their experienced in domestic relations matters to work for you.

If you call (888) 888-8888 today, they will waive their standard hourly fee for your initial consultation. This offer also applies if you mention this commercial while visiting their new office to arrange an initial consultation.

At that consultation, the attorneys can determine the fairness of your award of alimony, child custody, or visitation in a divorce, as well as similar matters."

Will the attorneys be subject to discipline?

A.   No, if their conduct complies with the contents of their commercial.

B.   No, because their commercial does not target people who are either represented or unrepresented by other counsel.

C.   Yes, because they are seeking, as prospective clients, people with whom they lack any existing relationship.

D.   Yes, because a person must mention the commercial to obtain a free initial consultation when the person visits the new office to arrange that consultation.

QUESTION #99

A prosecutor files charges against a defendant in a criminal case. An attorney serves as the defendant's defense counsel in a bench trial before a judge. The trial raises novel issues of law and fact regarding criminal liability for drug offenses involving a chemical substance that was similar to a legally prohibited controlled substance. The parties do not provide expert testimony regarding the novel issues.

At the close of the case, the judge informs the parties that he will render a judgment as soon as possible. The prosecutor becomes concerned that the judge's possible delay in rendering a decision might violate the local speedy trial rule. That rule does not authorize any *ex parte* communication during the proceeding. The prosecutor writes a letter to the judge. The letter mentions the prosecutor's concern and offers to provide additional pleadings or expert testimony if necessary to assist judge in making a decision. The prosecutor does not send a copy of this letter to the attorney. The next day the judge renders the judgment.

Was the prosecutor's letter to the judge proper?

A.   No, because it constituted an *ex parte* communication during the proceeding.

B.   No, because the judge rendered the judgment the day after the prosecutor wrote the letter.

C.   Yes, because if the prosecutor reasonably believed that a violation of the local speedy trial rule could have occurred.

D.   Yes, because the prosecutor's letter did not seek to influence the judge's decision.

QUESTION #100

State law permits an attorney to maintain a law practice while serving part-time as a county commissioner in a county of the state. State law provides that if the county's commissioners authorize the construction of a new courthouse and the funding of 50% of its construction cost, the state will provide the other 50% of the funding. A contractor is a regular contributor to the attorney's campaign for the position of county commissioner. The contractor's business is being prosecuted for fraudulent charges in a case over which a judge is presiding. The judge sits on the bench in a courthouse that needs to be replaced because of its size and originally poor construction. As instructed by the contractor, the attorney writes a letter to the judge. The letter states that as a county commissioner, the attorney would be willing to support funding for a proposed new courthouse if the contractor's case is timely scheduled on the docket.

Will the attorney be subject to discipline?

A.   No, because the attorney wrote the judge pursuant to the contractor's instructions.

B.   No, because state law allows the attorney to maintain his part-time law practice while serving as a commissioner.

C.   Yes, because the judge could find the contractor not guilty on all charges.

D.   Yes, because the attorney's letter sought to influence the judge in the contractor's case.

QUESTION #101

An attorney agrees to represent a contractor as a plaintiff in a breach of contract lawsuit against a government defendant. The attorney and the plaintiff execute a retainer agreement specifying the hourly billable rate. The controlling law does not provide governmental immunity for this type of lawsuit. The attorney's litigation of the case both exhausts the plaintiff's retainer and involves additional billable hours for which the plaintiff has not paid the attorney. A jury returns a judgment awarding the plaintiff $75,000 in damages, which the defendant does not appeal.

The defendant sends a check to the lawyer satisfying the judgment. The attorney places the defendant's payment of damages in the client trust account and invoices the plaintiff $10,000, the amount due for unpaid billable hours of work. The attorney calls the plaintiff and informs the plaintiff of the amounts of the damage award and the invoice. The plaintiff replies that it would only pay $7,000 because it considered that sum to be reasonable. The attorney issues a $65,000 check to the plaintiff and moves $10,000 from the client trust account into the attorney's general account.

Will the attorney be subject to discipline?

A.   No, because the plaintiff must pay the attorney pursuant to their agreement.

B.   No, because the attorney paid the undisputed amount to the plaintiff and invoiced the plaintiff for $10,000.

C.   Yes, because the attorney and the plaintiff dispute the amount owed.

D.   Yes, because the attorney must receive the amount stated by the client and bring a claim for the balance.

QUESTION #102

Two attorneys, a family law attorney and a criminal defense attorney, enter into an association to practice law for profit. Later, they properly convert their organizational status to a professional corporation. They designate the family law attorney's wife, who is not an attorney, as their professional corporation's president. She has no direction or control of the attorneys' professional judgment. The family law attorney serves as the professional corporation's vice-president and is a shareholder. The criminal defense attorney serves as the professional corporation's secretary and is a shareholder. The criminal defense attorney's husband serves as an office assistant in the firm. The family law attorney and the criminal defense attorney decide to add another attorney to their firm in order to handle its growing case load. They interview and offer a salaried associate attorney position to a new lawyer, which does not make him an officer, shareholder, or member of the professional corporation. When they make this offer of employment, the family law attorney and the criminal defense attorney disclose their status as officers, shareholders, or members, along with the fact that the professional corporation's president is not an attorney.

Will the new lawyer be subject to discipline for accepting this offer of employment?

A.   No, because the lawyer was not an officer, shareholder, or member of the professional corporation and only held the status of a salaried employee.

B.   No, because the president neither directs nor controls the professional judgment of the family law attorney, the criminal defense attorney, or the new lawyer.

C.   Yes, because the family law attorney 's wife is the professional corporation's president.

D.   Yes, because the criminal defense attorney's husband serves as the firm's office assistant.

QUESTION #103

A judge is an incumbent member of the state court of appeals. The judge is up for re-election in the voting district where an attorney lives. The attorney is considering whether to be a candidate for a judicial office. If the attorney decides to be a candidate, he would run against the judge to win the seat. The attorney seeks to discover if any grievances were filed against the judge and/or if the judge has been disciplined for judicial misconduct. In response to the attorney's proper inquiry, the state judicial conduct commission provides a letter on official stationary indicating that, as a result of two grievances, the commission imposed discipline for one instance of judicial misconduct. Based in part on this letter's information, the attorney decides to run for election. During his campaign, the attorney uses this letter's information in a public speech. It is subsequently brought to his attention that the commission imposed discipline for two instances of judicial misconduct.

The existence of grievances and the commission's determinations are a matter of public record.

Will the attorney be subject to discipline for making an incorrect statement about the commission's imposition of discipline?

A.   No, because the attorney did not knowingly misrepresent any fact concerning the judge.

B.   No, because in a contested election the attorney can make any statement about the judge.

C.   Yes, because the typographic error in the letter cannot excuse the attorney's false statement of a material fact.

D.   Yes, because the judge was disciplined for two instances of judicial conduct.

QUESTION #104

An attorney usually represents clients pursuant to a retainer agreement. A plaintiff, a musician, suffers a serious loss of income when a defendant, a music company, fails to pay the plaintiff any royalties on the music he wrote and performed. In order to obtain the attorney's services without initially providing any funds, the plaintiff suggests a contingency fee arrangement. The plaintiff offers to make payments to the attorney of 10% of the royalties that the defendant pays to the plaintiff after the plaintiff prevails against the defendant in this civil action to receive royalties. The plaintiff proposes that the attorney would recover her legal fees and litigation expenses from these payments by the plaintiff. The attorney agrees to pursue a civil action for the plaintiff against the defendant pursuant to those terms.

Will the attorney be subject to discipline based on this agreement?

A.   No, because the plaintiff requested the agreement's terms and conditions.

B.   No, because the attorney and the plaintiff can agree to a reasonable contingency fee.

C.   Yes, because the attorney obtained a proprietary interest in the plaintiff's civil action.

D.   Yes, unless the attorney's total fee is not greater than that which she could have obtained by billing a reasonable hourly rate.

QUESTION #105

An attorney worked for a law firm prior to being elected to the state legislature. Once elected, the attorney resigns from the firm. He serves in the state legislature for three two-year terms and cannot run for office again due to the state's term limit law. The attorney decides to go into private practice of law at the end of his final term. The attorney composes the following notice, which contains the attorney's name at the top of the notice, and pays for its publication in a daily legal newspaper:

"Following six-years of public service in the state legislature, I am returning to the practice of law. My new office is located in the Office Plaza, at 100 Central Avenue, City, State, 99999. Please feel free to call regarding questions or with requests for legal assistance. My number is (222) 222-2222."

Will the attorney be subject to discipline for publishing this notice?

A.   No, because the notice consisted of true statements.

B.   No, because the notice did not include any information that was not otherwise publicly accessible.

C.   Yes, because the notice was published to people who had not been his clients.

D.   Yes, because the attorney's service as a legislator had no bearing upon his competence as a lawyer.

QUESTION #106

A law firm employs a supervising attorney and a subordinate attorney. The supervising attorney is responsible for oversight of the work of the subordinate attorney. The law firm represents a product manufacturer who has been sued in a products liability action. The supervising attorney instructs the subordinate attorney to review their client's documents and identify any of them having legal significance. The subordinate attorney provides copies of the legally significant documents to the supervising attorney, who reviews and returns those copies with instructions that the subordinate attorney destroy certain original versions of those documents. The subordinate attorney complies with the supervising attorney's instructions.

Will the subordinate attorney be subject to discipline for complying with the supervising attorney's instructions?

A. No, because the subordinate attorney had a duty to obey the supervising attorney's instructions.

B. No, because neither the supervising attorney nor the subordinate attorney violated any ethical rule.

C. Yes, because the supervising attorney violated an ethical rule.

D. Yes, because the subordinate attorney cannot avoid responsibility for violating an ethical rule by obeying the supervising attorney's instructions.

QUESTION #107

An attorney is an active member of a non-profit organization. The organization's purpose is to rescue, shelter, and protect victims of domestic abuse. The attorney maintains a law office as her full time occupation. Her general law practice includes criminal defense work. The attorney serves as an appointed attorney for criminal defendants in some of the local courts in the jurisdiction where she is admitted to the bar. The attorney incurs significant expense when representing criminal defendants for which a court appoints her as defense counsel in a small number of assigned cases. A court seeks to appoint the attorney to represent a defendant during his prosecution for repeated and severe instances of domestic abuse. The attorney strenuously objects to this appointment on the basis of her personal beliefs and membership in the organization. The attorney asserts that, based on the charges against the defendant, she cannot represent him.

Will the attorney be subject to discipline for seeking to avoid being appointed to represent the defendant?

A. Yes, because the attorney must represent everyone she is appointed to represent.

B. No, because representing the defendant could impose a financial burden upon the attorney.

C. No, because representing the defendant will probably violate an ethical rule.

D. No, because the defendant is so repugnant to the attorney as to probably impair their client-lawyer relationship or her ability to represent him.

QUESTION #108

A prospective client calls a criminal defense law firm. The prospective client meets with an attorney in the firm for an initial screening interview. In response to his request for representation at an arraignment in 10 days, the attorney in the firm takes the prospective client's paperwork and tells him not to be concerned about the arraignment. In the next eight days, neither the attorney nor the law firm respond to the prospective client, who does not contact them or any other defense counsel to request representation. The attorney calls the prospective client back on the ninth day and refuses to represent him. The attorney has no reason for denying the representation.

Will the attorney be subject to discipline for refusing to represent the prospective client?

A.   No, because no client-lawyer relationship could arise from an initial screening interview.

B.   Yes, because an attorney has a duty to represent a client who requests representation.

C.   Yes, because a client-lawyer relationship existed between them based on detrimental reliance.

D.   No, because the attorney can always refuse to represent any client who requests representation.

QUESTION # 109

A manufacturer contacts an attorney seeking representation in a business dispute with a distributor. The attorney agrees to represent the manufacturer and they execute a valid written retainer agreement. During the attorney's representation of the client, they discover that the dispute involves a retailer. The attorney agrees to represent the manufacturer in the business dispute with respect to the retailer as well as the distributor. Because the disputing parties fail to make any compromise or settlement agreement, the manufacturer instructs the attorney to commence litigation against both the distributor and retailer. During the course of litigation, one year after they made their agreement, the attorney incurs some unexpected increases in her costs of doing business. The attorney seeks to enter into another contract modifying their agreement by increasing her hourly billable rate from $125 to $150. Initially, the manufacturer objects to the modification, but then agrees to it in order to continue the attorney's representation.

Will the attorney be subject to discipline?

A.   Yes, because the attorney changed her billing rate during term of the representation.

B.   Yes, because the manufacturer initially objected to the change in billing rate.

C.   No, because the attorney experienced increases in her business costs.

D.   No, because the attorney communicated the billing rate increase and the manufacturer agreed to it.

QUESTION #110

An attorney resides in a house on street that has a commercial business on its corner. The attorney is personal friends with the owner of the business.

A prospective client meets with the attorney. During their initial meeting and interview, the prospective client explains that he provided certain services to the owner's business for which the owner has not compensated him. The prospective client has invoiced, called, and written the owner to request payment several times. The prospective client has received no promises or assurances of payment from the owner. The prospective client requests that the attorney represent him on a contingency fee basis whereby the attorney would recover a reasonable and legally permitted percentage of the amount of funds that the owner owes to the prospective client.

Will the attorney be subject to discipline for declining to represent the prospective client?

A.   No, because an attorney can always refuse to represent any prospective client for any reason.

B.   No, because the attorney's personal friendship with the owner may negatively impact his relationship with the prospective client as a client.

C.   Yes, because the attorney has a duty to represent every prospective client.

D.   Yes, because the attorney's personal friendship with the owner will not adversely affect his relationship with the prospective client as a client.

QUESTION #111

An attorney works in a small firm and mainly practices domestic relations law and probate law. The attorney is the granddaughter of a prospective client and they have known each other since her childhood. The prospective client visits the attorney's office because he is seeking her probate law services. He requests that she prepare his last will and testament. As her client, he wants the will to include, in addition to its usual terms and conditions, certain bequests to his family members and friends. Specifically, the client instructs the attorney to include a bequest to the attorney of a classic automobile.

Will the attorney be subject to discipline if she prepares the will as instructed?

A.   No, because an attorney can prepare a will for a client giving a substantial gift to herself if the gift is made knowingly and voluntarily.

B.   No, because the attorney can prepare, for the client, a will giving the attorney a substantial gift because they are relatives.

C.   Yes, because the attorney cannot prepare for any client an instrument giving a substantial gift to herself.

D.   Yes, because the attorney cannot prepare, for the client, a will giving a classic automobile to the attorney because they are relatives.

QUESTION #112

A mortgagee (lender) retains an attorney to represent its interests in a commercial real estate deal. A mortgagor (borrower) requests a special business loan for funds to acquire a parcel of real estate and construct a skyscraper on the parcel. The loan will be secured by a mortgage on the parcel and the skyscraper. The loan and mortgage documents will be complicated. If they are incorrectly drafted, it could prevent the mortgagee's interest from being properly secured. The mortgagee will process the loan if the attorney drafts the loan and mortgage documents and the mortgagor pays the attorney's costs for this work. This approach is common in this situation of skyscraper development where the attorney works. The attorney reasonably believes that he can provide both the mortgagee and mortgagor with competent and diligent representation. They both provide written consent to the representation after each having consulted with independent lawyers.

Is it proper for the attorney to prepare the loan and mortgage documents?

A.   No, because the mortgagor, not the mortgagee, will pay the attorney.

B.   No, because the interests of the mortgagor and the mortgagee are different.

C.   Yes, because both the mortgagor and the mortgagee provided informed consent to the attorney's representation.

D.   Yes, because this approach is common where the attorney works.

QUESTION #113

In response to an attorney's advertisement, a client stops by an attorney 's office and schedules an initial consultation. After the client consults with the attorney, they execute a valid retainer agreement setting the attorney's hourly rate at $150. The attorney allows the client to mail in a $9,000 retainer check. Before the check arrives, the attorney performs 10 hours of work on the client's matter.

After receiving the check, the attorney places it in her client trust account. Next, the attorney moves $3,000 of the client's retainer into her general account. The $3,000 consists of $1,500 as her legal fees for the initial 10 hours of work, and $1,500 for work the attorney legitimately expects to perform (another 10 hours) on the client's matter on the following day. The attorney, however, only works five hours on the matter before the client calls her the next day. The client informs the attorney of a change in the situation as a result of which the attorney does not need to spend further time on the matter. Consequently, the attorney moves $750 from the general account back into the client trust account and retains the remaining $750 of the $1,500 as legal fees for services rendered.

Will the attorney be subject to discipline?

A. No, because the attorney moved the $750 that she did not earn from the general account back into the client trust account.

B. No, because the attorney legitimately expected to perform another 10 more hours of work on the client's matter the next day.

C. Yes, because the attorney withdrew $1,500 before completing all legal work for the client.

D. Yes, because the attorney moved $3,000 of the retainer into the general account when she had only earned $1,500 in legal fees.

QUESTION #114

An attorney works in a law firm that primarily represents corporate clients in business matters. The majority of the attorney's practice involves drafting, reviewing, and enforcing commercial landlord-tenant agreements. The attorney receives notice of a recent change in the law governing such leases that will affect the lease that the attorney drafted three years ago for a client, whom the attorney no longer represents. The attorney contacts the client to inform it of the change in the law and the resulting necessity of modifying the lease.

Will the attorney be subject to discipline for soliciting employment?

A. No, provided the attorney does not subsequently prepare a new lease for the client.

B. No, because the attorney formerly represented the client.

C. Yes, if the attorney possessed any basis to think that the client obtained other counsel.

D. Yes, because the attorney would be soliciting legal business from someone other than a current client.

QUESTION #115

An attorney is a high-profile criminal justice law specialist and author. The attorney testifies in a state legislative committee's fact-finding proceeding. He gives opinion testimony, both as an individual and an expert regarding state criminal justice issues. He does not, however, reveal that he is appearing on behalf of a paying client that has contracts with the state to operate state correctional facilities.

The attorney's testimony corresponds with his client's position on the issues, which the attorney personally considers to be good public policy.

Did the attorney properly give the testimony and not reveal his client's name?

A. No, because an attorney cannot receive compensation for attempting to affect legislative action.

B.   No, because an attorney who testifies before a legislative body needs to disclose the role in which the attorney appears.

C.   Yes, but only if the attorney sincerely thought that he advanced a position that served the public interest.

D.   Yes, because the legislature is concerned with the nature of the testimony rather than the source of a witness' compensation.

QUESTION #116

An attorney is a sole practitioner whose general law practice involves a variety of issues. The attorney prepares the paperwork for the formation of a business partnership by two partners. The attorney reviews and drafts other legal documents for the partnership. Subsequently, the partner s meet with the attorney and explain a business situation that concerns them. The attorney informs them that this situation could give rise to criminal liability, and that he could not assist them in the furtherance of any criminal conduct. The partners request that the attorney jointly represent them.

The attorney advises them that he would consider the request and let them know if he could assist them. The attorney sends a separate letter to each partner informing each that the partners might be better served by separate attorneys rather than the same attorney. The attorney also informs them that he would represent them both so long as they were equally involved in, and responsible for, the situation. The letter further states that he might need to withdraw from the representation if a conflict of interest develops between the partners, or if either of them does not want to continue with the dual representation. In that event, they both would need to obtain new legal representation. The attorney explains that he would be equally representing them without a preference for either partner. The attorney also makes clear that any communications by the partners would not remain confidential amongst each other. The partners execute and return the attorney's original letter and representation agreement setting forth these terms.

Did the attorney agree to this dual representation on proper terms?

A.   No, because the attorney's dual representation was conditional upon the waiver of client-lawyer confidentiality by both partners.

B.   No, unless the attorney provided the partners with notice that they should contact independent counsel before signing and returning their letter to him.

C.   Yes, if the risk that the interests of either partner would be materially prejudiced by the dual representation was not significant.

D.   Yes, because the attorney had already been representing both partners with respect to their partnership.

QUESTION #117

A contracts attorney's practice primarily consists of contracts law work. The contracts attorney drafts a sales contract for a seller, who sells recreational vehicles. The contracts attorney and her secretary witness the execution of the contract by the seller and the purchaser. Two weeks after the purchaser bought the recreational vehicle, a proper judicial proceeding resulted in a determination finding the purchaser mentally incompetent. Consequently, a conservator was appointed to manage the purchaser's legal and financial affairs. The conservator retains a litigation lawyer who files a lawsuit against the seller seeking to avoid the contract between the seller and the purchaser. The lawsuit alleges that the purchaser lacked the requisite mental capacity to enter into the contract when he executed it.

The seller asks the contracts attorney to defend him against the conservator's lawsuit. The contracts attorney's secretary and the seller died before the contracts attorney decided whether to represent the seller. Pursuant to a local rule, the seller's legal representative was substituted in his place as a proper party to this lawsuit. The seller's legal representative renewed the seller's request that the contracts attorney provide legal representation in this lawsuit. The contracts attorney remains the sole person who witnessed the contract's execution. In the contracts attorney's opinion, the purchaser was mentally competent when he executed the contract and thus possessed the mental capacity to enter into it. The contracts attorney is willing to testify about that if necessary.

Will it be proper for the contracts attorney to agree to represent the seller's legal representative?

A.   No, because the attorney may be called to testify regarding a contested issue.

B.   No, because the attorney drafted the contract that gave rise to the lawsuit.

C.   Yes, because the attorney is the only attesting witness still alive.

D.   Yes, because the attorney can testify regarding a contested issue.

QUESTION #118

An attorney represented a client for twenty years. The attorney prepared the client's will. The attorney and the attorney's receptionist acted as the two subscribing witnesses to the will's execution. The will provided 5 percent of the client's estate to her best friend, 15 percent to her daughter (who was the client's only heir), and the residue was left to a charity the client volunteered for during her lifetime. The will appointed the client's accountant to act as executor. The client died one year after the will was executed. The accountant named as executor in the will asked the attorney to represent her through the probate process. The client's daughter believed that the client suffered from mental illness during the last few years of life. The daughter informed the accountant the she planned to challenge the validity of the will on the grounds of mental incapacity. The attorney disagrees with the daughter's assertion. The attorney reasonably believes that the client was fully competent during the attorney's entire relationship with the client, leading up to the client's death. The attorney plans to testify about the client's mental capacity if called as a witness in the action. The attorney's receptionist at the time of will execution, who acted as the other subscribing witness to the will, fled the country to evade unrelated criminal charges and has not been found despite a diligent effort by law enforcement authorities.

Would it be proper for the attorney to represent the accountant for the will probate action?

A.   No, because the attorney's testimony relates to a contested issue.

B.   No, because the client's daughter, as surviving heir, obtains the benefit of the fiduciary duty to the client by the attorney.

C.   Yes, because the attorney is the only available subscribing witness to the will's execution.

D.   Yes, if the attorney makes a good faith effort to locate the receptionist.

QUESTION #119

An attorney, who is a sole practitioner, runs a general practice, but is rapidly gaining a reputation for her work in family law matters. The attorney has just been ordered by the court to represent a criminal defendant who has been charged with embezzling thousands of dollars of state-issued funds from the orphanage where he worked. The money he allegedly stole was earmarked for providing medical treatment to several children at the orphanage with chronic illnesses. The local newspaper has published several opinion pieces denouncing the defendant since his arrest, and two television stations are providing continuing news coverage of the case.

The attorney has handled serious criminal matters before, and is confident that she could ably represent the defendant, despite her strong distaste for the crime with which he has been charged. However, she is worried that, given the extensive news coverage of the case, there is a chance that her association with a defendant who people believe stole from orphans will harm her reputation and cause potential clients with family law matters to seek out other attorneys. The attorney has not yet met with the defendant or entered an appearance on his behalf.

May the attorney decline the court's request that she represent the defendant?

A.   Yes, because she strongly dislikes the crime the defendant is charged with committing.

B.   Yes, because she has not yet established an attorney-client relationship with the defendant.

C.   No, because the mere possibility that new clients will not hire her does not create an unreasonable financial burden.

D.   No, because she has not first obtained the defendant's informed, written consent to decline the representation.

QUESTION #120

A well-reputed divorce lawyer has been contacted by a wife to represent her in divorce proceedings. The wife, who is unemployed, is taking care of her two children alone and living in a motel because her husband refused to leave their house or take care of the children. The wife has explained that her husband has withdrawn hundreds of thousands of dollars out of their bank accounts and, as a result, she cannot access any funds to pay the attorney a retainer. The wife is worried that if she does not take legal action soon, her husband will spend or hide all of their money, leaving her unable to take care of their children.

The lawyer is a seasoned divorce attorney who feels that the wife has been wronged by her husband. The lawyer wants to help the wife and agrees to represent her without a retainer. Because he is confident that he can secure a divorce, child support, and a sizeable alimony award for the wife, the attorney insists on his usual rate of $400 per hour, plus costs, to be paid at the end of the divorce proceedings. Less experienced attorneys in their city charge approximately $350 per hour for similar work. The lawyer's fee will be due regardless of whether the husband and wife actually divorce, and regardless of the ultimate division of their assets. At the end of the initial consultation, the attorney puts the fee agreement in writing and both he and the wife sign it.

Is the fee agreement between the lawyer and the wife proper?

A.   The fee agreement is proper because the lawyer's fee is reasonable.

B.   The fee agreement is improper because the lawyer's agreement to accept payment at the end of the proceedings amounts to a contingency fee.

C.   The fee agreement is proper because even though the lawyer is charging a contingency fee, the agreement has been reduced to writing and the wife has provided written consent to the agreement by signing it.

D.   The fee agreement is improper because the lawyer's $400 per hour fee is *per se* unreasonably high.

QUESTION #121

A lawyer represented the owner of a local restaurant in a labor dispute with several of his waiters over unpaid wages. During the representation, the lawyer reviewed all of the owner's accounting books and business practices, and learned that the owner underpaid all of his employees. The lawyer detested working with the owner, but he did a good job and the matter was resolved in the owner's favor several months ago, thus ending the lawyer's representation of the owner. A group of busboys from the restaurant (who were not party to the suit by the waiters) are now claiming that the owner refuses to pay them overtime wages. The busboys have contacted the lawyer to represent them in a suit against the owner. To ensure that he complies with his ethical obligations, the lawyer calls the owner and explains that he has been contacted by the busboys and would like to take on the representation. The owner says that he didn't like working with the lawyer and couldn't care less if he represents the busboys. The owner then hangs up on the lawyer.

Which of the following best describes the lawyer's ability to represent the busboys?

A. The lawyer may not represent the busboys because the representation would involve a concurrent conflict of interest, which has not been waived by both parties.

B. The lawyer may not represent the busboys because he has not obtained the owner's informed, written consent.

C. The lawyer may represent the busboys because he is no longer representing the owner and the owner consented to the representation.

D. The lawyer may not represent the busboys because he obtained information during the previous representation that could be damaging to the owner in the busboys' lawsuit.

QUESTION #122

A small law firm recently hired an associate who graduated from law school the previous summer and who was just admitted to the bar. The associate, who has only been with the firm for a few weeks, has been fulfilling his duties at the firm under the supervision of the managing partner. Because the firm cannot afford much support staff, the associate has been given a number of administrative tasks, such as going through the mail and conducting firm business at the bank. The managing partner has thoroughly trained the associate to handle these tasks in compliance with the Model Rules of Professional Conduct.

Yesterday, the associate opened a letter that included a sizeable check made out to the firm as a settlement in one of the firm's cases. The associate immediately showed the check to the managing partner. The partner explained that he was relieved to receive the check, as business had slowed unexpectedly and the firm needed the money to pay some outstanding bills. He instructed the associate to take the check to the bank and deposit it. The partner stated that he would prepare an accounting for the client. The associate dutifully took the check to the bank, where he deposited it in the firm's operating account so that the firm could pay its bills right away.

Which of the following best describes the extent to which the associate and managing partner are subject to professional discipline?

A. Neither attorney is subject to discipline.

B. The managing partner is subject to discipline, but the associate is not.

C. The associate is subject to discipline, but the managing partner is not.

D. Both attorneys are subject to discipline.

QUESTION #123

A local entrepreneur has developed a business idea designed to capitalize on the recent influx of immigrants into his community. He intends to open up an immigrants' resource center, which will provide various cultural services otherwise unavailable to its patrons, such as connecting them with local religious and civic organizations, as well as employment opportunities, for a nominal fee. The center will also serve as a platform for local businesses, which are struggling in the slow economy, to advertise their services – for a more substantial fee. The entrepreneur consults with a local immigration attorney to see if he would be interested in purchasing advertising space at the center. The attorney explains that he not only wants to advertise at the center, but that he would like to help finance the project. In exchange, he wants the center to exclusively refer its clients with legal issues to his practice. The entrepreneur is thrilled, as having the lawyer's financial assistance will eliminate some of his own risk in developing the business, and agrees to the attorney's proposal, provided that he will refer his clients to the resource center. The two agree to develop the resource center as partners, and open it for business only a few weeks later.

Is the lawyer subject to discipline based on his agreement with the entrepreneur?

A. No, because none of the services provided by the resource center constitute the practice of law.

B. No, because there are no ethical restrictions on lawyers entering into lawful business relationships.

C. Yes, because a lawyer may not enter into a partnership with a non-lawyer.

D. Yes, because the referral agreement between the lawyer and entrepreneur is improper.

QUESTION #124

While driving home from work one afternoon, a personal injury attorney witnessed a car accident caused when a driver in a luxury sedan ran a red light. After running the light, the sedan swerved to avoid another vehicle and sideswiped a station wagon. Not one to miss a business opportunity, the attorney hurried over to the accident scene and approached the station wagon. The attorney recognized the injured station wagon driver as a local probate lawyer with whom she had a mutual acquaintance. An ambulance arrived and, as the paramedics helped the station wagon driver, who had suffered some minor injuries, into the ambulance, the attorney handed her his business card and, with all sincerity, explained: "I saw that guy run a red light. Let me take your case and I'll help you sue the pants off of him." Before the driver of the station wagon could respond, the paramedics shooed the attorney away as they loaded her into the ambulance and sped off to the hospital.

While at home recovering from her injuries, the station wagon driver found the personal injury attorney's business card and, remembering the attorney's crass, tasteless behavior during a moment when she was vulnerable, she became incensed. An attorney herself, the station wagon driver considered professional ethics to be of the utmost importance. Hoping to teach the personal injury attorney a lesson about professional behavior, she decided to report his conduct to the state bar.

If the station wagon driver reports the personal injury attorney to the state bar, will he be subject to discipline for soliciting her as a client?

A.   Yes, because lawyers may not directly solicit business from individuals for pecuniary gain.

B.   No, because the driver of the station wagon is a lawyer.

C.   No, because he witnessed the accident and reasonably believed he could win the case.

D.   Yes, because the driver of the station wagon did not want him to solicit her business.

QUESTION #125

One of a firm's named partners, who also helped found the firm, was elected to the state legislature, and he has been in office for the past six months. By law, a state legislator may hold private employment, provided that the private employment does not create a conflict of interest with a legislator's duties. Because the partner's firm is located in the state capital, and the legislature is regularly out of session, the partner has been able to remain involved in most of his cases, although he occasionally solicits help from other partners when his legislative duties require it. Moreover, the partner has dutifully avoided any conflict of interest between his legal practice and his official duties in the legislature. Since the partner began his duties in the state legislature, no action has been taken to remove the partner's name from the firm's name.

Given the above facts, which of the following most accurately describes the obligations of the firm and its partners under the Model Rules of Professional Conduct?

A.   The partner may not serve as both a practicing attorney and a public official, and his name must be removed from the firm's name as long as he remains a legislator.

B.   The partner may continue to practice with the firm while he is in the legislature, but his name must be removed from the firm's name.

C.   The partner cannot continue to practice with the firm while he is in the legislature, but his name can remain part of the firm's name because it is his legacy.

D.   The partner may continue to practice with the firm, and the partner's name may remain in the firm's name.

QUESTION #126

A business owner contacted an attorney about representing him in negotiations to acquire a competitor's business. The attorney, who had only been in practice for a short time, agreed to take on the representation and asked how the business owner got his name. The businessman explained that he was a friend of the attorney's neighbor, who had recommended him.

The negotiations took several weeks, earning the attorney a handsome $25,000 fee. The attorney was grateful to his neighbor for the referral and, as thanks for sending some business his way, showed up on the neighbor's doorstep with a $50 bottle of wine – paid for with money earned from the representation. The neighbor told the attorney that he didn't have to get him anything, but the attorney insisted, explaining that it was the least he could do for sending him such a lucrative job opportunity.

Is the attorney subject to discipline for giving the wine to his neighbor?

A. Yes, because he has split the client's fee with a non-lawyer.

B. No, because he gave his neighbor a reasonable gift in exchange for the referral.

C. Yes, because the lawyer cannot compensate his neighbor for the referral.

D. No, because the value of the gift was substantially less than the fee obtained from the client.

QUESTION #127

A prominent lawyer is on the board of directors of, and owns shares of stock in, his family's business: a company that produces medical devices. The other members of the board include the lawyer's parents, his wife, and his two sisters. The company, which is headquartered in a state on the east coast, is currently mired in state court litigation there (and only there), resulting from both regulatory actions by the state government and consumer suits. Although he serves on the board of directors, the lawyer's participation is minimal, requiring only a few days of his time each year. The lawyer lives in a state on the west coast, where he has just been appointed to the state judiciary.

Assuming that he will not violate any other provisions of the Model Code of Judicial conduct, which of the following best describes the new judge's obligations under Model Code of Judicial Conduct Rule 3.11?

A. The judge may hold the company's stock and remain on the board of directors because the company is closely held by the judge and his family members.

B. The judge must resign from the board of directors and sell off his company stock because the company is frequently involved in state court litigation.

C. The judge may keep his company stock, but must resign from the board of directors because his participation will necessarily interfere with his judicial duties.

D.   The judge must sell off his stock and resign from the board of directors because he may not participate in a business with non-lawyers.

QUESTION #128

A lawyer is representing a husband in divorce proceedings. The lawyer prides himself on helping divorcing couples get through the divorce process as amicably as possible, and has had great success doing so in the past. The wife's divorce attorney, on the other hand, is known for aggressively representing his clients' interests to get them the largest possible award. The parties held negotiations, and the husband's lawyer was doing his best to deal with the wife's combative attorney, who has become nearly impossible to deal with. During a recent meeting with his attorney following negotiations, the husband became extremely emotional and stated that he had no interest in getting a divorce and just wanted to reconcile with his wife. The lawyer felt that this provided an opportunity to use his skills and, with his client's approval, immediately phoned the wife at home. He explained that she should speak one-on-one with her husband, who still loved her and wanted to reconcile. Moved by the attorney's words, she agreed and told the lawyer to send her husband over to talk. The following day, the couple reconciled and the wife withdrew the petition for divorce.

Is the husband's lawyer subject to discipline for calling the wife?

A.   The lawyer is not subject to discipline because his phone call was made in his client's best interest and with the client's approval.

B.   The lawyer is not subject to discipline because the lawyer's conduct was reasonably calculated to advance his client's interest, and the wife assented to the phone call.

C.   The lawyer is subject to discipline because he contacted the wife without first obtaining her lawyer's authorization.

D.   The lawyer is subject to discipline because a lawyer may never directly contact an adverse party who is represented by counsel.

QUESTION #129

A woman was involved in a late-night car accident several months ago. Although neither she nor her 18-year-old son, who was in the car with her, was badly hurt, the driver of the other vehicle involved in the accident suffered a serious injury. The other driver then sued the woman, so she hired a lawyer to represent her. Although her son is likely to serve as a witness, he was not named as a defendant in the action. While the lawyer was interviewing the son to learn more about the accident, the son explained that he thought that the accident was his mother's fault. The son explained that he thinks his mother may have been falling asleep at the wheel. The lawyer asked the son not to volunteer that information to anyone else – especially the lawyer for the other driver – unless he is required to do so under oath.

Is the lawyer subject to professional discipline for his request to the son?

A. No, because the son is related to the lawyer's client.

B. Yes, because the son is not the lawyer's client.

C. Yes, because the other driver is entitled to know the truth.

D. No, because the son's communication is privileged.

QUESTION #130

A lawyer represents the owner of a bookstore in a contract dispute with the owner's former business partner. During the course of the proceedings, tensions have run high and the two parties, who were once close friends, have become bitter enemies. At two settlement conferences, the owner and his former partner almost engaged in fistfights, and all attempts to resolve the matter peacefully so far have failed. Because of the stress caused by the lawsuit, the owner's health and ability to manage his business have taken serious hits. Concerned for his client's health and well-being, the lawyer suggested that the owner offer his former partner an extremely generous settlement, cut his losses, and focus on fixing his business. The owner reluctantly agreed and the lawyer conveyed a substantial settlement offer to the former partner's attorney. The offer was ultimately rejected and the lawyer went to the bookstore to tell his client the bad news in person. The two spoke privately in the back office and, when the owner found out that his offer had been rejected, he became incensed. He removed a handgun from his desk drawer and said to the lawyer, "I'll show that jerk. This stays between you and me." The owner then fled the bookstore and sped off in his car.

Under the Model Rules of Professional Conduct, which of the following best describes how the owner's lawyer may proceed with regard to his client's statements and actions at the bookstore?

A. He may not contact the authorities.

B. He must contact the authorities.

C. He must seek permission from bar counsel before contacting the authorities.

D. He may contact the authorities.

QUESTION #131

The judge presiding over a civil jury trial invited the attorneys for the plaintiff and the defendant to her chambers to discuss an evidentiary issue outside of the jury's presence. While the judge and two lawyers were discussing the matter, the judge's clerk interrupted to tell the plaintiff's attorney that his client needed to speak with him urgently. When the plaintiff's attorney left (with the judge's permission), the defendant's attorney asked the judge if she would be amenable to taking a longer lunch break that day so that the attorney could appear before another judge in an unrelated matter. The judge said that she would agree, provided that it did not present a problem for the plaintiff's attorney. When the plaintiff's attorney returned to chambers, the judge told him that the defendant's attorney had asked for an extended lunch break to take care of another matter. The plaintiff's attorney objected to the request. Pursuant to state law, the court on which the judge sits permits lawyers to contact judges or their staff concerning scheduling issues without first contacting opposing counsel.

Are the defendant's attorney and/or the judge subject to discipline for having a discussion after the plaintiff's attorney left the room?

A.   Only the attorney is subject to discipline because he initiated the ex parte communication.

B.   Neither the attorney nor the judge is subject to discipline because their ex parte conversation was permissible.

C.   Neither the attorney nor the judge is subject to discipline because their conversation was not actually ex parte.

D.   Both the attorney and the judge are subject to discipline because ex parte communications are never permissible.

QUESTION #132

A lawyer represents a homeowner in an action against a neighbor. The homeowner has alleged that the resident has, for year after year, decorated his home with an inordinate number of holiday lights, causing him to lose sleep because of their brightness; the homeowner wants a court to enjoin the neighbor from continuing his garish light display, as well as damages. The homeowner's attorney called the neighbor to see about scheduling a settlement negotiation. When the neighbor answered the call, the attorney identified himself as the homeowner's representative, explained that he was hoping to set up a settlement conference, and asked if the neighbor had retained a lawyer who the attorney could speak with. The neighbor explained that he had no interest in hiring an attorney, that the complaining homeowner had been harassing him for years, and that he was considering countersuing for harassment. The homeowner's attorney then advised the neighbor that he should consider obtaining a lawyer, but that, in his experience, the neighbor did not have a viable claim for harassment. Given the facts of the case, the attorney reasonably believed that the neighbor did not have a viable harassment claim.

Is the attorney subject to discipline for his interaction with the neighbor?

A.   Yes, because he advised the neighbor about the merits of a possible harassment suit.

B.   Yes, because he contacted the neighbor, who was not represented by counsel.

C.   No, because the attorney reasonably believed that the neighbor's proposed countersuit lacked merit.

D.   No, because the neighbor explained that he had no interest in hiring a lawyer.

QUESTION #133

A lawyer successfully represented a real estate developer in having a land parcel in a residential neighborhood re-zoned to accommodate the developer's proposed condominium. The re-zoning was the only matter the lawyer handled for the developer, and no other lawyer in his firm did any work for the developer. The condominium was completed several years ago, and a number of its residents have approached the lawyer about representing them in an action against the developer for defective construction.

Can the lawyer represent the condominium residents?

A.   Yes, because the tenants' interests are not materially adverse to those of the real estate developer.

B.   Yes, because the tenants' case is unrelated to the lawyer's work on the zoning issue.

C.   No, because he has not obtained the developer's informed, written consent.

D.   No, because the tenants' interests are materially adverse to those of the developer.

QUESTION #134

Following his arraignment on homicide charges, the defendant in a high-profile murder trial was released after posting a substantial bond. On the day jury selection was set to start, the defendant panicked and fled the state. When news got out that the defendant had fled, the prosecutor assigned to the case decided to hold a press conference. At the conference, the prosecutor declined to answer specific questions from members of the press. Reading a brief, pre-written statement, the prosecutor explained that police were investigating the defendant's whereabouts, that anyone with information about the defendant's location should contact the police, and that, because the defendant's flight was clear evidence of his guilt, anyone encountering the defendant should exercise caution.

Is the prosecutor subject to discipline for his press conference statement?

A.   No, because he provided information concerning public safety.

B.   No, because the prosecutor did not represent the defendant and had an adversarial role in the proceedings.

C.   Yes, because he spoke publicly about an ongoing criminal proceeding.

D.   Yes, because his statement was likely to prejudice potential jurors against the defendant.

QUESTION #135

A lawyer recently became a sole practitioner when his former partner split from their firm following a disagreement about the management of the practice. The former partner opened up his own firm, hired several associates, and had begun directly competing with the lawyer for clients. Hoping to build up his one-lawyer practice to stay competitive, the lawyer offered a job to a corporate attorney with a sizeable book of business. Still angry about the way he had been treated by his former partner, the lawyer included a provision in the corporate attorney's contract stating that, if the corporate attorney should leave the firm, she would not work for the former partner in any capacity.

Is the contract provision permissible?

A.   Yes, because there are no restrictions on a law firm's ability to limit the professional conduct of its employees.

B.   Yes, because the restriction on the corporate attorney's future practice is reasonably calculated to avoid an actual conflict of interest.

C.   No, because it restricts the right of the corporate attorney to practice law.

D.   No, because it was proposed by the employer, not the employee.

QUESTION #136

A judge is considering hiring his niece, a recent law school graduate, to serve as his clerk. His niece graduated at the top of her class, previously interned for a judge in the state in which she attended law school, and published a law review article while serving as articles editor on her school journal. Of the three hundred applications the judge has considered, she is among the three most qualified candidates.

Can the judge offer his niece the clerkship?

A.   No, because she is a family member within the third degree of relationship.

B.   Yes, because members of the judiciary have absolute control over administrative appointments.

C.   Yes, because the judge's niece is an exceptionally qualified applicant.

D.   No, because the judge could only hire her if she was the most qualified applicant.

QUESTION #137

A lawyer has decided to change the focus of his practice from family law to immigration and citizenship law. He has handled only one immigration case before, but has studied immigration and citizenship law extensively and is reasonably confident that he will be an effective immigration attorney. To drum up business, the lawyer places an advertisement in the local newspaper for his services. The ad contains the lawyer's name, office address, and phone number, and reads: "Specializes in Immigration and Citizenship Matters." No organization in the state in which the attorney practices certifies attorneys as "specialists" in legal subject matters.

Is the attorney subject to discipline for his advertisement?

A. Yes, because he may not indicate that he is a specialist if he has not been formally certified as a specialist.

B. Yes, because only attorneys practicing admiralty or patent law may identify themselves as specialists.

C. No, his advertisement is permissible.

D. Yes, because he has only handled one immigration case before.

QUESTION #138

A college fraternity wishes to recognize several of its prestigious alumni by hosting a free dinner in their honor. To ensure that there is enough space to accommodate everyone, the fraternity's president rents a dining hall at a fancy private club that opened recently. The fraternity has never conducted business with this club before. Unbeknownst to the fraternity's president, the club has an unwritten policy against African-Americans joining as members. Several members of the fraternity are African-Americans, as are some of the honorees who will be in attendance. Among the honorees invited to the dinner is a judge. The judge, who is white, is also unaware of the club's policy regarding African-Americans. He has never visited the club.

Will the judge violate the Code of Judicial Conduct by attending the dinner?

A. No, because the club is a private institution and it can therefore discriminate in accepting members.

B. No, because the dinner is an isolated event.

C. Yes, because the club discriminates on the basis of race.

D. Yes, because the judge has accepted the gift of a free dinner.

QUESTION #139

After a long, successful career, a sole practitioner passed away. His daughter was named the executrix of his estate, and the lawyer's will provided that his practice should be sold, if possible, so that the proceeds could be used to support his wife, who had always been a homemaker. The daughter, who was not a lawyer herself, arranged to sell her father's practice to a reputable local attorney. The purchasing attorney agreed not to raise the fees charged to the practice's existing clients. After all of the father's clients were properly notified of the proposed sale, the attorney paid the daughter, serving as the executrix, an agreed upon price for the practice. The daughter then gave the proceeds of the sale to her mother, as directed by the will. All of the father's clients agreed to keep their business with the purchasing attorney.

Was the sale of the deceased lawyer's practice proper?

A.   No, because the attorney who purchased the firm entered into the transaction with the daughter, who was not an attorney.

B.   No, because the proceeds of the sale went to a non-lawyer.

C.   Yes, but only because all of the father's clients kept their business with the purchasing attorney.

D.   Yes, regardless of whether the father's clients kept their business with the purchasing attorney.

QUESTION #140

A law firm in the city devotes part of its practice to the representation of corporations that own and manage rental apartments. In addition to his work with the law firm, an associate at the firm serves on the board of directors of the local legal aid organization, which provides free assistance to low-income individuals in a wide variety of civil matters, such as landlord-tenant disputes and employment discrimination suits. In fact, some of the organization's attorneys have represented clients in actions against the associate's corporate clients.

The legal aid organization has had its budget slashed recently and it cannot continue to devote its resources to a wide variety of cases. Another member of the board of directors has proposed that the organization seek to withdraw from representing its clients in current landlord-tenant disputes, which often require much of an attorney's time and which rarely have a broad impact on society. Some of the organization's clients are currently involved in landlord-tenant disputes with the associate's clients; the associate is aware of that fact. The board of directors is preparing to vote on the proposal.

Which of the following best describes the associate's obligations under the Model Rules of Professional Conduct?

A.   The associate may continue to serve on the board of directors, but he may not participate in the vote.

B.   The associate may continue to serve on the board of directors and he may participate in the vote.

C. The associate should resign from the board of directors and decline to participate in the vote.

D. The associate must report his participation with the legal aid organization to the state bar association because his participation violated the Rules of Professional Conduct.

QUESTION #141

One of a firm's named partners was elected to serve as the state's attorney general. By law, the attorney general may not hold private employment. The partner is a founder of the firm and has been a named partner since the firm's inception. If the firm changes its name, it will incur substantial costs in replacing all firm marketing materials, building signage, as well as a billboard in downtown.

Given the above facts, which of the following most accurately describes the obligations of the firm and its partners under the Model Rules of Professional Conduct?

A. The partner may not serve as a practicing attorney in any capacity while he is the attorney general, and his name must be removed from the firm's name as long as he remains a public official.

B. The partner may not continue to be a partner, but may serve as "of counsel" to the firm, while he is the attorney general, but his name must be removed from the firm's name.

C. The partner cannot continue to practice with the firm in any capacity while he is the attorney general, but his name can remain part of the firm's name because it is his legacy.

D. The partner may continue to practice with the firm, and the partner's name may remain in the firm's name.

QUESTION #142

An attorney represents a client, a defendant, involved in litigation concerning a construction dispute. The client is a builder with a good business reputation throughout the state. The client has been sued by a customer who alleges that the home builder defectively constructed a gazebo in the customer's backyard. The gazebo collapsed under the weight of four children. One of the children, the customer's son, was severely injured.

The attorney hires a recent graduate of a prestigious local paralegal training educational program. The paralegal graduated as the valedictorian of the most recent class. The attorney prepared an answer to the complaint and directed the paralegal to file the answer on the day it was due. The paralegal negligently failed to file the answer.

The court enters a default judgment in favor of the plaintiff as a result of the failure to timely file an answer.

Which of the following correctly states the attorney's professional responsibility?

A. The attorney is subject to discipline on the theory of respondeat superior.

B. The attorney is subject to discipline if the attorney failed to adequately supervise the legal assistant.

C. The attorney is not subject to discipline because an attorney is not responsible for the negligence of a non-attorney.

D. The attorney is not subject to discipline if the attorney personally was not negligent.

QUESTION #143

An attorney noted for her expertise in First Amendment law has been asked by a federal appellate court to represent an indigent litigant in a civil appeal presenting complicated free speech issues. The attorney, who is listed on a register of lawyers willing to accept pro bono appointments in federal criminal and civil cases, is the most qualified attorney on the list to handle the matter, though there are certainly other competent attorneys available. The appeal involves the litigant's right to publicly promote the ideas of a group that vehemently opposes religious minorities. The lawyer is a member of such a religious minority and, although she has never personally faced problems because of her religious affiliation, she grew up hearing stories of her grandmother's escape from religious persecution, and she cannot bear the thought of representing someone who would endorse the kind of suffering her grandmother endured.

Which of the following best describes the attorney's responsibilities under the Model Rules of Professional Conduct?

A. She must accept the representation because she is presumed competent to handle the matter.

B. She may seek to decline the representation because representing an unpopular client will create an unreasonable financial burden.

C. She may seek to decline the representation because she strongly opposes the litigant's views.

D. She must accept the appointment because the court requires her expertise in the subject matter of this case.

QUESTION #144

A lawyer maintains a trust account at the local bank for one of his clients. Because the amount held in trust is fairly small, the bank imposes a monthly service charge of $1.99. To ensure that the service charge is covered, the lawyer deposits money from his operating account into the client trust account each month. Out of an abundance of caution, the lawyer makes each monthly deposit in the amount of $2.99. By doing so, the lawyer makes sure that the service charge never eats into the client funds held in trust. The lawyer always keeps detailed records related to his deposits to the client trust account.

Is the lawyer subject to discipline for the way he manages his client trust account?

A. Yes, because he deposits more of his money in the trust account than is needed to pay the maintenance fee.

B. Yes, because it is never permissible to mix a lawyer's money with client trust money.

C. No, because the deposits from the lawyer's own account exceed the maintenance fee, thereby protecting the client's entrusted funds.

D. No, because the lawyer maintains properly detailed records identifying which funds in the client trust account are his.

QUESTION #145

A lawyer is being paid by a businessman to represent the businessman's son in divorce proceedings. The son has given informed consent to his father's payment of the lawyer. The businessman is concerned that his son's estranged wife will take advantage of the son's generous nature, and he is especially concerned that the son will give up several valuable family heirlooms to secure an amicable divorce, but will ultimately regret such a decision. At the businessman's request, the lawyer agrees to terminate any settlement negotiations if it appears that the son is likely to give his wife any of the family heirlooms. The lawyer informs the son of his agreement with the businessman. The son explains that his only concern is making sure that his marriage ends as peacefully as possible.

Can the lawyer honor his agreement with the businessman?

A. Yes, because the businessman is paying for the attorney's services.

B. Yes, because the businessman's request is reasonably intended to benefit his son.

C. No, because the lawyer has agreed to an improper contingency fee.

D. No, because the agreement limits the lawyer's ability to exercise his own judgment.

QUESTION #146

A young man, down on his luck, has been charged with trying to cash bad checks, a criminal offense. Although he is financially eligible for court-appointed counsel, the young man does not believe a public defender will adequately represent him, so he contacts a private attorney. He explains to the attorney that he was recently laid off from work and that he only passed the bad checks because he was destitute and needed to find a way to keep food on his table without drawing on the small amount of money he has saved. The attorney feels bad for the young man, but is facing tough times herself, as she has had trouble finding new clients. To achieve a balance in their interests, the attorney cuts the young man a deal: she will represent him for her usual fee, which amounts to a substantial portion of the young man's savings, but will only collect the fee if the young man is acquitted of the criminal charges.

Is the attorney's proposed fee agreement permissible?

A. No, because it is a contingent fee.

B. Yes, because the fee is reasonable under the circumstances.

C. Yes, because the young man will not have to pay if he is convicted.

D. No. The attorney must take on the young man's case *pro bono* because he is an indigent defendant.

QUESTION #147

Over the past several years, two friends – a tax attorney and an accountant – have worked out a beneficial deal. In exchange for the accountant referring legal matters to the tax attorney, the tax attorney refers business to the accountant. Although the accountant refers his clients only to the tax attorney, the tax attorney knows a number of good accountants, and he tries to distribute his referrals evenly among them. The attorney has decided that he doesn't want clients to think that he is only referring business to this particular accountant simply on the basis of their friendship, but rather because the accountant is good at his job. Accordingly, the tax attorney intentionally conceals the fact of their friendship from clients that he refers to the accountant, though he does explain that they have a practice of referring clients to one another.

Is the tax attorney subject to discipline for his referral agreement with the accountant?

A. Yes, because he does not disclose his friendship with the accountant to clients he refers to the accountant.

B. No, even though he does not disclose his friendship with the accountant.

C. No, because there is no restriction on reciprocal referral agreements between lawyers and non-lawyers.

D. Yes, because the attorney has not agreed to refer clients exclusively to a single accountant.

QUESTION #148

An attorney represents a business owner being sued by a former employee for gender discrimination. The former employee is represented by a lawyer, but is not happy with the lawyer's failure so far to make progress in the case. Frustrated, the former employee calls the business owner's attorney and informs him that she is tired of waiting for her lawyer to take action and will settle her case for $10,000 – far less than she requested in her civil complaint. The business owner's lawyer tells the former employee that he will relay her offer to his client.

Which of the following correctly states the responsibility of the business owner's lawyer under the Model Rules of Professional Conduct?

A.   The business owner's lawyer is subject to discipline because he did not alert the former employee to the significant difference between her settlement offer and the amount requested in her complaint.

B.   The business owner's lawyer is subject to discipline because he agreed to convey the former employee's offer to his client.

C.   The business owner's lawyer is not subject to discipline because the former employee initiated the phone call.

D.   The business owner's lawyer is not subject to discipline because he did not give the former employee any legal advice.

QUESTION #149

Several members of a family suffered serious injuries in a car accident due to a design flaw in their vehicle. They obtained the help of a lawyer, who has managed to make a very strong case on their behalf against the auto manufacturer. The lawyer has proven very skilled and was able to uncover information about the car's design process that, if revealed at trial, would certainly score a victory for his clients and probably expose the auto manufacturer to significant liability in other cases. To help avert a disaster, the attorneys for the auto manufacturer have presented the family with an extraordinarily high settlement offer. In exchange, the manufacturer insists that the damaging information be kept confidential and that, given his unique knowledge of the case, the family's lawyer may not thereafter represent plaintiffs alleging design defects in the car model at issue.

Which of the following best explains the obligations of the family's lawyer under the Model Rules of Professional Conduct?

A.   The lawyer may agree to the proposed settlement because he has managed to obtain an unexpectedly high settlement offer, which is in his clients' best interests.

B.   The lawyer may agree to the proposed settlement because it is functionally equivalent to a victory for his clients at trial.

C.   The lawyer may not agree to the proposed settlement because it would be unethical to do so if the family is certain to win at trial.

D. The lawyer may not agree to the proposed settlement because it restricts his ability to represent other plaintiffs raising similar claims.

QUESTION #150

A young attorney wishes to open his own for-profit law practice, but he has substantial law school debt and cannot afford the startup costs on his own. His father, an accountant, offers to loan the attorney the money he needs. The father will not be a partner in the firm. However, the father is concerned that if the attorney takes any client who walks through the door, less scrupulous clients will fail to pay after legal services are rendered, and neither the attorney nor his father will see the money they are owed. To help insure his investment, the father insists on having veto authority over clients for the attorney's first six months of practice: if it appears to the father that a potential client is unlikely to pay agreed-upon fees after services are rendered, the attorney must decline the representation. According to their agreement, however, the father unequivocally gives up any such "veto" authority after six months have passed.

Is the attorney's agreement with his father permissible under the rules governing professional responsibility of lawyers?

A. Yes, because the father does not own a financial interest in the firm.

B. No, because the father can dictate which representations the attorney takes on.

C. Yes, because the father's "veto power" expires after a definite period.

D. No, because the father and his son have not formed a partnership.

AMERIBAR BAR REVIEW

MPRE Practice Questions

ANSWERS AND EXPLANATIONS

QUESTION #1

C is the correct answer in this permissive withdrawal situation. Under MRPC 1.16(b)(5), an attorney may withdraw from representation if the attorney's client fails substantially to satisfy an obligation to the attorney regarding the attorney's services and has been given reasonable notice that the attorney will withdraw unless the obligation is satisfied. Although the agreement gives the client notice of the possibility of withdrawal, the attorney would still need to give the client notice that he was going to invoke the clause because the client would need time to seek new counsel. Keep in mind, though, that the attorney may need to obtain permission of a court. In any event, the attorney must take steps to protect the client's interests.

A is a wrong answer because it is too categorical and failure to pay for services is an explicitly listed reason for permissive withdrawal. Likewise, B is wrong because, although attorneys should afford their clients the opportunity to execute certain types of agreements between them after consulting with some other lawyer, this is not the question's dispositive issue. Answer D is wrong because it does not cover all of the requirements for withdrawal, particularly that the attorney warned the client that the attorney intended to withdraw unless the obligation was fulfilled.

QUESTION #2

B is the correct answer in this client-lawyer confidentiality situation. MRPC 1.6 provides that a the attorney may not reveal information relating to the representation of a client unless (1) the client gives consent, (2) disclosure is required in order to carry out the representation, or (3) the disclosure falls within six specific categories. Here, the client specifically ordered the attorney not to fill out the form, and because the dispute is settled, disclosure is not required to carry out the litigation. Therefore, because the state's law does not require attorneys to complete the form, no basis exists for the attorney's disclosure here.

C is a wrong answer because disclosure would not be proper even if the attorney's work product is not revealed. A is an incorrect answer because disclosure of this information is not subject to a best interest standard, and the client's best interest is not one of the six situations where an attorney must reveal confidential information. D is a wrong answer because the duty of confidentiality continues even after the attorney ceases representing the plaintiff.

QUESTION #3

B is the correct answer to this question regarding the filing of baseless or frivolous pleadings. Both Federal Rule of Civil Procedure 11 and MRPC 3.1, the Rule requiring meritorious claims and contentions, require that an attorney base a pleading's claims on existing law. Here, the repeal of the federal statute caused the attorney's complaint to lose its support by existing law. But the attorney's timely compliance with Rule 11 by means of filing a valid amended complaint cured that violation. A is a wrong answer because it is not based on those legal provisions. C and D are incorrect because they do not state valid grounds for a litigation sanction.

QUESTION #4

B is the correct answer in this conflict of interest situation. The attorney cannot accept the employee as a client because his former employment by the department disqualifies him from representing her after his involvement in the handbook's development and disagreement with the attorney general. No facts indicate that the attorney sought or the department provided consent to his representation of the employee in a manner that would be directly adverse to the department. Accordingly, C and D are incorrect. A is wrong because the attorney cannot reveal to the employee the confidential information about the disagreement because the department is his former client.

QUESTION #5

C is the correct answer because it accurately states the dispositive reason that would subject the attorney to discipline. Contingency fee agreements are prohibited in both criminal cases and domestic relations matters. Here, the attorney improperly entered into such an agreement that would transfer real property to him if he achieved the client's objectives in her divorce action. D is a wrong answer because it is not the dispositive issue based on these facts. A and B incorrectly answer "yes" based on irrelevant reasons.

QUESTION #6

D is the correct answer because the advertisement will subject the attorney to discipline because it is misleading or false. MRPC 7.1 provides that attorneys may not make false or misleading communications about their legal services. A communication is false or misleading if it contains a material misrepresentation of fact. Here, the advertisement stated that attorney had a perfect trial win record when she actually lost one trial. Although she won on appeal of the case, her advertisement made a material misrepresentation of fact -- that she had a perfect trial win record -- because she lost one trial. A communication is false or misleading if it omits a fact necessary to make the statement considered as a whole not materially misleading. Here, the attorney's advertisement left out the fact that she lost one trial, which is required to make her statement about her trial win record, considered as a whole, not materially misleading. Because the attorney's advertisement made a false communication about her services, it was improper under MRPC 7.1. As such, A is a wrong answer because it states the opposite as D. B is not correct because principles of constitutional freedom of speech do not protect attorney advertisements that are false or misleading. Thus, C is incorrect because it is not the most on-point answer, although it is an accurate with respect to the attorney's false or misleading advertisement.

QUESTION #7

A is the correct answer because it accurately applies the relevant rule to these facts. The gift could arguably be incident to the wife's business and could reasonably be perceived as intended to influence the judge in terms of the owner's action against the builder. B is wrong because the owner's giving of the same gift to the builder would not mitigate the fact that the judge should not accept the gift under the Rule. C is incorrect because a business relationship is not required to prohibit the receipt of a gift by the judge. D is incorrect because judges can only accept gifts under limited circumstances.

QUESTION #8

D is the correct answer because the attorney's conduct violated MRPC 1.3, which requires the attorney to act with reasonable diligence and promptness in representing the plaintiff. The attorney's failure to file a mediation summary or motion to set aside the default, and her vacation before filing the motion to set aside the default judgment, shows a lack of diligence and promptness in prosecuting the plaintiff's case against the defendant. Thus, the attorney lacked a good cause for and meritorious defense to the default. Consequently, the court properly denied her motion to set aside the default. Accordingly, answers B and C are incorrect. A is a wrong answer because the dispositive issue is the attorney's lack of diligence and promptness and she cannot affect her liability

QUESTION #9

A is the correct answer because the attorney did not violate any pertinent rule of professional conduct and acted reasonably in declining the representation. MPRE 1.1 requires that an attorney provide competent representation to clients, which requires thoroughness and preparation reasonably necessary for the representation. Here, the attorney knew that she would not have the time to properly prepare for the individual's case, so she recommended that he meet with another lawyer. She also indicated that the individual needed to meet with other counsel quickly in order to preserve his enforcement right. Although factually accurate, B is a wrong answer because the attorney must still act reasonably in declining the representation. Thus, A is a more dispositive and definitive response. C and D are incorrect because no civil liability arises from these facts. With regard to C, the facts do not indicate that the attorney's advertisement was either false or misleading as she engages in transactional work, and she is only recommending that the individual seek different counsel because she does not have time to competently work, not because she did not perform that kind of work. With respect to D, the attorney had no duty to give the individual notice of the statute of limitations, and she performed all of her duties when she suggested that he needed to meet with another lawyer quickly.

QUESTION #10

C is the correct answer because it follows the Rule permitting the attorney to disclose the otherwise confidential fax in order to address the defendant's allegations in the disciplinary proceeding regarding the attorney's representation of the plaintiff. Generally, MRPC 1.6(a) prohibits an attorney from revealing information obtained while representing a client. MRPC 1.6(b) permits such revelation under certain conditions. These conditions include revealing the information "to respond to allegations in any proceeding concerning the lawyer's representation of the client." Although it relates to a valid Rule, D is a wrong answer because arguably the plaintiff's testimony perpetrated a fraud on the judge. A is an incorrect answer because the general rule of client-lawyer confidentiality is subject to an exception that is controlling under these facts. B is a wrong answer for the same reason, regardless of whether the plaintiff could be prosecuted for perjury. Under these facts, it is likely that he could be prosecuted for perjury.

QUESTION #11

C is the correct answer for two reasons. First, the Rule describing what constitutes professional misconduct, MRPC 8.4, includes instances of dishonesty such as misrepresentation. Second, MRPC 8.5 provides that regardless of where the attorney's misconduct occurs, she is subject to the disciplinary authority of state one. Indeed, she is subject to the disciplinary authority of both state one and state two. Thus, B is an incorrect answer because she is subject to discipline in both states. D is an incorrect answer because the Rules do not require that the attorney be convicted of a crime in the other state in order for her to be subject to discipline in her home state. A is a wrong answer because the attorney was licensed as an attorney when her misconduct occurred, and the Rules contemplate that misconduct that may lead to discipline may occur while an attorney is not serving in that capacity.

QUESTION #12

B is the correct answer because the Rules require that the attorney inform the defendant of the grandfather's payment offer before getting the defendant's consent to keep and use the grandfather's check. Specifically, MRPC 1.8(f) permits an attorney to accept compensation from someone other than the client if (1) the client consents, (2) the third party does not interfere with the attorney's independent use of her professional judgment, and (3) the attorney does not reveal confidential client information to the third party. A is a wrong answer because the Rules do not prohibit the grandfather from paying the attorney for representing the defendant. C is an incorrect answer because, although factually accurate, the Rules do not allow the attorney's defense of the defendant to be influenced by the grandfather. Moreover, that is a less dispositive provision of the Rules than their "informed consent" requirement. D is a wrong answer because it is factually inaccurate.

QUESTION #13

D is the correct answer because the client only consented to the original hourly rates in the retainer agreement, which the parties had not modified. Moreover, the attorney failed to communicate the changed hourly rates to the client, and MRPC 1.5(b) requires the attorney to communicate any changes in the fees to the client. C is a wrong answer because the fact that the retainer agreement was in writing does not subject the attorney to discipline when the Rules require that agreement to be written. Additionally, the parties may modify a written retainer agreement if the attorney communicates the change to the client. A is an incorrect answer because the client's lack of consent, not reasonableness of the hourly rate increases, is the dispositive issue. B is a wrong answer because the retainer agreement's requirement that the client pay hourly rates does not necessarily apply to the increased hourly rates.

QUESTION #14

C is the correct answer because by making false statements to the cashier, the lawyer violates the MRPC 8.4, which makes dishonesty and misrepresentation professional misconduct. Additionally, these statements are false partly because the attorney represents that the communications will be confidential when in fact the cashier's interests are adverse to those of the corporation. In that situation, under Comment [10] of MRPC 1.13, the discussions may not be privileged. D and B are incorrect answers because the dispositive issue is the attorney's false statements, not her dealing with the cashier as an unrepresented person. However, the attorney likely should have advised the cashier of the advisability of retaining counsel. A is a wrong answer because the lack of potential legal proceedings is not the controlling issue. Note that if the attorney obtained any incriminating statements from the cashier, she might have done that in a way that violated the cashier's rights.

QUESTION #15

D is the correct answer because the attorney cannot represent the individuals after her substantial participation in representing the department for one year, particularly here when no facts indicate that she has sought or received the department's written informed consent to this new representation. MRPC 1.11 mandates that a former government attorney may not, without first obtaining the consent of his former government agency, represent a client in connection with a cause of action with which the attorney "personally and substantially" participated while employed by the government. C is a wrong answer because the facts show that the final judgment was not completely dispositive of the corporation's liability, and that fact is not dispositive in this case. A is an incorrect answer because, regardless of the attorney's competence in this legal subject matter, she must obtain the department's informed consent to represent the individuals as clients. For the same reason, B is an incorrect answer even if there is no issue of confidentiality to the extent that the department made its data available to the public.

QUESTION #16

A is the correct answer because it provides the best option in terms of the facts and Rules. Pursuant to MRPC 1.5(e), the attorney and the lawyer could only make a proper division of the fee between them in proportion to the services that they each performed. Also, MRPC 1.5(e) requires that the client agree to the share that each lawyer will receive and that the fee be reasonable, but neither of these is a problem in this situation. Although factually correct, B is a wrong answer because the controlling part of MRPC 1.5 does not mention that the amount must be the same, although presumably that would be the case here. C is a wrong answer because the client provided written consent as the Rules require. D is an incorrect answer because the fact that only the lawyer would try the case is not a relevant consideration under the Rules.

QUESTION #17

D is the correct answer. Comment [6] to MRPC 1.1 on Competence states: "To maintain the requisite knowledge and skill, a lawyer should keep abreast of changes in the law and its practice, engage in continuing study and education and comply with all continuing legal education requirements to which the lawyer is subject. " In a jurisdiction such as the home state, which does not require continuing legal education, an attorney can decline to participate in such courses. Still, an attorney has a duty of providing competent representation. As the comment above contemplates, that duty may only be satisfied by maintaining sufficient competence to handle legal matters, which can be accomplished by self-guided continuing legal education. C is a wrong answer because, although factually accurate, it does not address the dispositive issue of competence to practice law in the home state, where the dissenting attorney practices law. A is an incorrect answer because, as described earlier, the dissenting attorney could maintain legal competence without participating in the courses. B is a wrong answer because, although factually accurate, the firm's provision of malpractice insurance coverage does not make proper non-participation in the courses by the dissenting attorney.

QUESTION #18

B is the correct answer because the judge's failure to disqualify himself from presiding over the derivative action violates MCJC R 2.11(A). The Rule requires disqualification in a proceeding in which the judge's impartiality might reasonably be questioned. Here, the judge should know that the parties would reasonably question his impartiality if they knew that he owned many of the corporation's shares because a judgment could affect the value of the corporation and its shares. Under MCJC R 2.11(A)(2)-(3), a judge's impartiality might be reasonably be questioned, such that the judge must disqualify himself, when: 1) the judge knows that he has more than a *de minimus* interest that could be substantially affected by the proceeding; or 2) the judge knows that he has an economic interest in the subject matter in dispute or a party to a proceeding before the judge. Here, based on what the trustee told him, the judge knows that he has more than a *de minimus* interest in his many shares of the corporation's stock, the value of which the case could substantially affect. Therefore, the judge knows that he has an economic interest in the derivative action and the corporation it involves. Yet, the judge went forward with pre-trial proceedings despite knowing about his economic interest in their subject matter or the corporation, the defendant in them.

A is an incorrect answer because disclosure of the interest is insufficient. Although C and D are factually accurate, they do not provide reasons why the judge would not be subject to discipline.

QUESTION #19

D is the correct answer. MRPC 7.1 requires that any advertisement for an attorney or lawyer must not contain "false or misleading communications about the lawyer or the lawyer's services" and defines "false or misleading" as a communication that "contains a material misrepresentation of fact or law, or [that] omits a fact necessary to make the statement considered as a whole not materially misleading." If the attorney and the lawyer both possess those referenced degrees, then their advertisement is truthful. If they did not possess those degrees, though, then their advertisement would be false and misleading in violation of the Rules. C is a wrong answer because the fact that only law is a licensed profession is irrelevant. A is an incorrect answer because whether the appearance of L.L.M. and Ph.D. in the advertisement is superfluous is irrelevant. B is a wrong answer because the permissibility of the advertisement's reference to L.L.M. and Ph.D. does not depend upon restriction of the firm's practice to the subject matter for which those degrees are needed.

QUESTION #20

C is the correct answer. MRPC 1.1 imposes on an attorney the mandatory duty of competence to his or her client, which requires "the legal knowledge, skill, thoroughness and preparation reasonably necessary for the representation." An attorney who is incompetent in his or her representation may be subject to discipline. Here, the attorney did not know about, and failed to take heed of the judge's information about, the criminal penalties to which the witness would be subject if she refused to testify. Therefore, the attorney continued to incorrectly advise her against testifying. This behavior shows a lack of the attorney's competence. B is an incorrect answer because the attorney's belief that the witness had a legal right not to respond to the question would likely not protect the attorney from discipline. The judge made such a belief unreasonable by informing the attorney of the law. A is a wrong answer because the fact that the witness followed the attorney's advice does not preclude the attorney's liability for discipline. Conversely, D is a wrong answer because the witness's violation of the law by following the attorney's counsel does not necessarily subject the attorney to discipline.

QUESTION #21

B is the correct answer. MPRC 8.1 provides that an attorney may not knowingly make a false statement of material fact on an application or "fail to disclose a fact necessary to correct a misapprehension known by the person to have arisen in the matter." Because the attorney did not know of the information when he completed the form, he would not have violated the Rules unless he learns of the information and fails to correct the mistake. A is not the best answer because it does not take into account that negative information that comes to light may need to be revealed. C is incorrect because the attorney may rely on representations if he reasonably believes the information. Finally, D is incorrect because at the time he did not know that the statements he was making were false.

QUESTION #22

D is the correct answer because MRPC 3.8 requires that the district attorney, a prosecutor, timely provide the accused's lawyer with all "exculpatory" evidence that the district attorney knows either tends to either negate guilt or mitigate the offense. Here, the district attorney failed to do that. Thus, B is an incorrect answer because the district attorney had a duty to initially disclose the additional evidence that was later discovered.

A is a wrong answer because the district attorney's duty to provide all exculpatory evidence is not contingent upon the lawyer's making an appropriate pretrial discovery request. C is an incorrect answer because, even if it describes a likely result, it is a less optimal response than D's reference to the controlling Rule.

QUESTION #23

B is the correct answer because the defendant's admission to the attorney about her fraudulent statements is a confidential communication, which is protected by the Rule of client-lawyer confidentiality. MRPC 1.6(a) makes it mandatory for an attorney to keep information relating to the representation of his or her client confidential unless the client gives informed consent. MRPC 1.6(b) provides six exceptions to the mandatory rule, under which the attorney may reveal confidential information, although he is not required to. Under these facts, the communication does not fall under any exception to this Rule, and the defendant has not consented to its disclosure. Thus, A is a wrong answer because the attorney would be maintaining the confidentiality of that communication by not providing notice of the fraudulent statements to the police. C and D are incorrect answers because the communication is not a basis for the attorney's withdrawal from representing the defendant. Note that because the attorney did not represent the defendant when she made the fraudulent statements, the attorney is not obligated to take reasonable remedial measures such as disclosure of those statements to the legislative committee.

QUESTION #24

A is the correct answer because the partner attorney recognized that the associate lawyer did not possess the competence to handle the company's case and she did not intend to sufficiently supervise him to protect the company's interest. MRPC 1.1 requires an attorney to provide competent representation to her client. Additionally, MRPC 1.16(d) states that upon terminating representation, an attorney must do what is "reasonably practicable" to protect the client's interest. Arguably, this principle applies here to the partner attorney's transfer of the case to the lawyer. B is a wrong answer because it provides a less dispositive reason, even if the attorney needed the company's consent to transfer the case to the lawyer. C is an incorrect answer because the associate lawyer's law license did not qualify him as having the legal competence to handle any type of case. Instead, the associate lawyer would need to gain sufficient competence to handle an antitrust law case through sufficient study and education. D is a wrong answer because the partner attorney cannot withdraw from any case solely on the basis that handling it would cause her substantial financial hardship. Further, the facts do not indicate either a withdrawal (but rather a transfer) or that any financial hardship existed.

QUESTION #25

C is the correct answer because the attorney knew that the defendant gave false testimony regarding her date of birth and the attorney failed to take reasonable remedial measures such as disclosure of that falsity to the tribunal. MRPC 3.3(b) imposes a duty upon an attorney in this situation to take appropriate remedial measures, including, if necessary, the disclosure of any known perjury. The defendant engaged in perjury by providing testimony under oath stating her false date of birth, instead of her true date of birth.

D is a wrong answer because whether the defendant violated the law by using a fake identification card is not the dispositive issue. A is a wrong answer because it would incorrectly allow the attorney to conceal the defendant's true date of birth on the basis of client-lawyer confidentiality. Here, however, the attorney is obligated to disclose that true date because he knew that a defendant engaged in fraudulent conduct by falsely stating the date in testimony. B is an incorrect answer because the defendant's real date of birth was an issue in the proceeding.

QUESTION #26

D is the correct answer because, under these circumstances, the attorney could make a permissive withdrawal from representing the client if the attorney complies with MRPC 1.16. Pursuant to MRPC 1.16(b), an attorney may withdraw if: 1) the client fails substantially to fulfill an obligation to the lawyer regarding the lawyer's services; and 2) the lawyer provides reasonable warning that the lawyer will withdraw unless the client fulfills the obligation. Here, the client substantially failed to fulfill the contractual obligation to pay the attorney for services rendered as invoiced. The attorney's invoices and letters provided the client with notice of this obligation, an opportunity to fulfill the obligation, and the possibility of the attorney's withdrawal for non-payment. Thus, B is a wrong answer because the conduct of the attorney and the client does support withdrawal.

C is an incorrect answer because the client's failure to pay the invoices does not require the attorney's withdrawal. Under these facts, the withdrawal is optional or permissive, rather than required or mandatory. A is wrong because the facts do not indicate that the contract is invalid.

QUESTION #27

C is the correct answer because the attorney should have deposited the check in a client trust account for the plaintiff, rather than her general account. Under MRPC 1.15, when an attorney receives funds belonging to a client, she should deposit those funds in a separate trust account for the client. Here, the check represented funds that belonged to the plaintiff because the defendant paid them in settlement of the trespass lawsuit. Thus, the attorney should have deposited the check in a separate trust account for the plaintiff before paying the plaintiff the $800 pursuant to their contingency fee agreement. Accordingly, A is not correct because the attorney deposited the check in the improper account. The fact that the case is over does not eliminate this requirement. For the same reason, B is a wrong answer even though it is factually correct.

Because the facts do not indicate that the plaintiff is disputing the amount due to the attorney, she properly deducted 20% from the $1,000 when issuing the check to the plaintiff. Alternatively, the attorney could have issued a $1,000 check to the plaintiff and then billed the plaintiff for $200. D is a wrong answer because the attorney deducted the correct amount of $200 and, as a practical matter, a 20% contingency fee is reasonable.

QUESTION #28

D is the correct answer because it applies a controlling Rule to these facts. MRPC 1.2 provides that the client has sole discretion for determining the objectives of the litigation. The Rule, though, places primary responsibility for the means of representation with the attorney. The attorney must, though, reasonably consult with the client regarding the means. The Rules are not clear as to how the parties should proceed if there is a conflict regarding how the attorney should represent the client, but MRPC 1.16 permits an attorney to withdraw, among other reasons, if the client has made representation unreasonably difficult, and the client is always entitled to fire the attorney. The attorney may need to provide notice or receive permission from the court to withdraw.

Thus, A is an incorrect answer because the attorney is not obligated to follow the plaintiff's directions regarding how he will represent the plaintiff. If, as here, the plaintiff is making it unreasonably difficult for the attorney to achieve those objectives, then withdrawal may occur upon motion, notice, and court approval. B is a wrong answer because, although factually accurate, the court can authorize the attorney's withdrawal even over the plaintiff's objections.

C is an incorrect answer because there are limits on when the attorney may withdraw before trial. The Rules provide for either mandatory or permissive withdrawal under certain circumstances.

QUESTION #29

D is the correct answer because it accurately applies the controlling Rule to these facts. MRPC 1.8(d) prohibits an attorney from making or negotiating an agreement with a client for media or literary rights "to a portrayal or account based in substantial part on information relating to the representation" prior to the resolution of the case. The comment to MRPC 1.8 states that the Rule is intended to prevent the possibility that the marketability or lack thereof of a certain outcome might inappropriately influence the attorney's decisions to the client's detriment. Accordingly, C is a wrong answer because an attorney may obtain such rights only after the representation's conclusion.

A is a wrong answer because application of MRPC 1.8(d) does not turn upon whether the defendant consults with another lawyer about making an agreement with the attorney regarding media or literary rights. Even if the defendant consults with another lawyer, the attorney could not make such an agreement with the defendant until after the case's conclusion. B is an incorrect answer because application of MRPC 1.8(d) is not limited to a lawyer's representation of a client in either a criminal or civil matter.

QUESTION #30

D is the correct answer because the attorney is improperly assisting the company in practicing law when the company lacks authority to do so. MRPC 5.5 governs when an attorney may practice law, and although it provides that the attorney may delegate some work to paraprofessionals under appropriate supervision, the comments to MRPC 5.5 make clear that it is intended to protect the public from receiving legal advice or services from an unqualified individual. C is a wrong answer because the agreement's limitation on the attorney's representation to only his own clients -- who do not present a conflict of interest to the company -- is different from a restriction on the right to practice prohibited under the Rules. The Rules are concerned with such a restriction that applies after a representation relationship ends.

A is a wrong answer because the attorney's provision of "free" service to the company's clients is not the dispositive issue, and he does not have to pay rent for using the company's office space. B is an incorrect answer because the attorney's lack of advising the company's clients does not negate his involvement in the company's unauthorized practice of law.

QUESTION #31

C is the correct answer because the statement is impermissible in this situation. MCJC R 2.10(B) prohibits a judge from making promises that are inconsistent with the judge's impartial performance of his adjudicative duties. The judge's statement improperly makes a promise about the issue of takings that may come before him if he is elected to the state supreme court. The statement is not consistent with the judge's impartial performance of official duties because the statement shows that he would not impartially adjudicate the issue.

Thus, D is incorrect because the judge may publicly discuss the topic, provided that the judge does this in compliance with the MCJC. A is wrong because, although a judge has a constitutional right of free speech, the MCJC limits the right under certain circumstances. B is not correct because, although immunity or privilege affords a defense to defamation claims against judicial officers, the defense does not apply here to shield the judge from discipline.

Note that the judge could have made some other proper statements on the topic during the debate. The MCJC permits judicial candidates to make general statements of opinion without being subject to discipline for making such statements. For example, in the context of this question's facts, the judge could have said: "It is my opinion that the state government is constitutionally authorized to take land if doing that is beneficial for economic development." Alternatively, the judge could have said: "I consider the issue of governmental takings to be a legitimate issue for the judiciary to resolve in its decisions."

QUESTION #32

C is the correct answer because it accurately applies the permissive withdrawal provision of the Rules to these facts. MRPC 1.16(b) permits an attorney to withdraw if the client insists on continuing with a course of action that the attorney reasonably believes is fraudulent or illegal. D is an incorrect answer because the mandatory withdrawal provision of these rules does not apply unless the attorney's continued representation of the company "will result in a violation of the Rules or other law." Here, the company's continuation of the potentially fraudulent activity is not dependent upon the attorney's continued representation. A is a wrong answer because it is irrelevant that, as the company asserts, the attorney's withdrawal would indicate that the filing is unlawfully flawed because the attorney's withdrawal is permitted in this situation. Although the Rule prohibits the attorney from withdrawing if doing so would have a "material adverse effect on the interests of the client, B is a wrong answer because the company's corporate counsel would still be able to correct the filing.

QUESTION #33

D is the correct answer because the lawyer can make comments about the attorney's temperament and qualifications as a potential judge, if they are based on his reasonable belief. Conversely, MRPC 8.2(a) prohibits the lawyer from making such statements about the qualifications or integrity of the candidate that he knows to be false or with reckless disregard as to their truth or falsity. Thus, A is a wrong answer because even if the lawyer's comments dishonored the judiciary, that alone does not render them improper. B is an incorrect answer because the Rule does not completely prohibit the lawyer from making public remarks regarding judicial candidates. C is a wrong answer because the Rule applies although the lawyer was not campaigning for judicial office.

QUESTION #34

B is the correct answer because the attorney violated the Rules by preparing the reporter to ask about the transaction. MRPC 5.3(c) states that an attorney will be responsible for any conduct of a non-lawyer employed by the attorney that would violate the rules if the attorney engaged in it. The reporter served as the attorney's agent in contacting the contract administrator. The corporate counsel represented the contract administrator as the company's employee. Because MRPC 4.2 prohibits the attorney from communicating with a represented person about the subject matter of the representation without the person's attorney's consent, the attorney -- through the reporter's actions -- engaged in unauthorized communication with a represented person without the corporate counsel's consent. A is an incorrect answer because the attorney could not have interviewed the contract administrator without the corporate counsel's consent. C is a wrong answer because the fact that the attorney fulfilled the plaintiff's request does not bring the attorney's conduct into compliance with the Rules. D is an incorrect answer because the fact that the answers obtained by the reporter contained evidence important to the plaintiff's action does not bring the attorney's conduct into compliance with the Rules.

QUESTION #35

B is the correct answer because it complies with MCJC R 2.9(A)(2), which states when the judge may obtain disinterested advice from an expert. The judge may obtain disinterested expert advice if: 1) there is full disclosure to the parties regarding the person the judge consulted and what the advice is; and 2) the judge gives the parties reasonable opportunity to respond. A is a wrong answer because the parties' advance written consent to the expert's advising of the judge does not fulfill the MCJC's controlling provisions. C is an incorrect answer because, although factually accurate, it only describes one of the provisions required for a judge to talk to a disinterested expert. D is a wrong answer because, although it states a practical reason to obtain the expert's advice, it is not a provision of the MCJC.

QUESTION #36

 D is the correct answer because misrepresentation is one type of misconduct that MRPC 8.4 prohibits. Although C is a factually correct statement, it is a wrong answer because it lacks the dispositive fact of the attorney's civil liability for misrepresentation. That fact may give rise to subjecting the attorney to discipline for professional misconduct. A is an incorrect answer because the Rules' description of misrepresentation as misconduct is not limited to either civil or criminal culpability for such misconduct. B is a wrong answer because no exception to the Rule against misrepresentation exists for allegedly doing that in the best interest of the seller as the attorney's client.

QUESTION #37

B is the correct answer because the question was not qualified or limited to any type of offense. MRPC 8.1 specifically prohibits a bar applicant from knowingly making a false statement of material fact. The applicant knowingly made a false statement of material fact by answering the question in the negative with respect to adult offenses when he knew that he had committed juvenile offenses. Thus, the question should have been answered in the affirmative despite the lack of adult offenses. A is a wrong answer, although it accurately states that the applicant did not contact the professional authority about the scope of the question's application. The applicant could have inquired of the authority about this to possibly avoid knowingly making a false statement of material fact, but this is not the reason he is subject to discipline. In other words, attempting to contact the authority would not relieve him of acting improperly. However, B is a better answer because it is the direct reason why the applicant is subject to discipline. C is an incorrect answer because the dispositive issue is whether the applicant knowingly made a false statement of material fact, not if he had a reasonable belief about the question's scope. The controlling Rule does not provide that a reasonable belief will excuse or justify making a false statement of material fact. D is a wrong answer because even if the applicant considered his answer to be an accurate statement of material fact regarding adult offenses, it was an inaccurate statement of material fact regarding juvenile offenses that he failed to disclose.

QUESTION #38

B is the correct answer because the attorney neither participated in nor knew about the office's investigation of the accused. MRPC 1.11 is clear in that a former government employee will only be disqualified from representing a client if he or she substantially and personally participated in representation of the same matter while working for the government. The former government employee's new firm will not be disqualified from undertaking the representation unless the employee is disqualified under the above provision. Accordingly, a conflict of interest would not exist with respect to the attorney and the accused that could be imputed to the lawyer to prevent him from accepting the accused as a client. A is a wrong answer because, although factually accurate, it states a less dispositive reason than answer B does for why the lawyer will not be subject to discipline. Although C is factually accurate, it is an incorrect answer because the attorney did not participate personally and substantially in the investigation of the accused. D is a wrong answer because it describes a provision of MRPC 1.11 that would apply only when a conflict of interest exists.

QUESTION #39

B is the correct answer because it provides the best option under the Rules and facts. Generally, MRPC 8.3(a) requires the lawyer to inform the professional authority of the attorney's violation of the Rules that raise a substantial question as to the attorney's honesty, trustworthiness, and fitness to act as a lawyer. Even if the attorney arguably violated MRPC 1.3 by his one-month delay in the couple's adoption matter, that does not necessarily raise a *substantial* question as to the attorney's honesty, trustworthiness, and fitness to act as a lawyer. Here, the attorney returned the retainer and the couple accepted his explanation for the relatively reasonable delay. Accordingly A and C are incorrect answers because they are too categorical in terms of whether or not the attorney violated the Rules such that the lawyer had to report that violation.

Moreover, pursuant to MRPC 8.3(c), a lawyer does not have to disclose information protected by MRPC 1.6, the Rule of confidentiality. Here, the couple wanted to keep confidential what they told the lawyer about the attorney's conduct. Thus, D is a wrong answer because arguably the lawyer properly complied with the couple's request and the Rules by not reporting the attorney's conduct.

QUESTION #40

B is the correct answer for two reasons in this legal fee dispute situation. First, the client is entitled to receive from the attorney that part of the retainer that was not needed for an appeal bond and there is no dispute as to who is entitled to those funds. Second, the client's request for a refund of the entire amount constitutes a dispute regarding the $1,500 in fees that the attorney earned (10 hours X $150). MRPC 1.15(d) requires that the attorney keep this disputed amount separate from other funds until the dispute is resolved. Thus, the attorney cannot move the $1,500 from the client trust account into her general account until that occurs.

A is a wrong answer because the attorney would violate the Rule by moving the other funds ($1,500) from the client trust account to her general account.

C is an incorrect answer because the attorney is not required to return the full retainer amount. The attorney may keep the funds in the client trust account subject to resolution of the dispute.

D is not a correct answer for two reasons. First, as explained earlier, the attorney issued the check in the correct amount because the attorney must return the unearned portion of the retainer, the $1,000 for an appeal bond, to the client. Second, the attorney correctly kept the remaining funds in the client trust account because moving $1,500 to her general account would violate MRPC 1.15(d).

QUESTION #41

D is the correct answer because it properly applies the relevant MCJC provision to these facts. MCJC R 3.8(A)prohibits judges from serving as a fiduciary except for members of their families when doing so will not interfere with their proper performance of judicial duties. A is a wrong answer because, of itself, the fact that the daughter is a federal judge does not prohibit her from serving as a fiduciary for her father, a family member. However, those facts could preclude her from serving in that capacity when additional facts show that doing so would interfere with her proper performance of judicial duties. B is a wrong answer because, although the father's family members could challenge the living will's validity, the facts state that their doing that is improbable. Moreover, their doing that would not necessarily interfere with the daughter's proper performance of her judicial duties. C is a wrong answer because, although the daughter is closer to the father than the son, that fact does not make the daughter's service as a patient advocate proper.

QUESTION #42

D is the correct answer because the prosecutor violated MRPC 3.5(a), which prohibits an attorney from seeking to influence prospective jurors by any means prohibited by law. The comment to this Rule indicates that such violations will be defined by either criminal law or the MCJC. Here, the facts state that the publicity resulted in biasing and prejudicing prospective jurors, contrary to applicable criminal law. C is a wrong answer because it is factually inaccurate. A is an incorrect answer because, even if it were factually accurate, it does not excuse the prosecutor's misconduct. Although it is factually true, B is a wrong answer because the prosecutor can violate the Rule by either directly or indirectly seeking to influence a prospective juror.

QUESTION #43

B is the correct answer because the attorney's advice: 1) attempted to prevent the defendant from violating the law by avoiding judicial proceedings and escape being apprehended; and 2) did not assist the defendant in doing that. MRPC 1.2(d) prohibits an attorney from helping a client in conduct that the attorney knows is criminal or fraudulent, but that prohibition does not extend to counseling a client as to the consequences that might flow from such action. Here, the attorney's conduct conformed to that Rule. A is incorrect because an attorney can be subject to discipline if the attorney assists a client in engaging in illegal or fraudulent conduct or advises the client to engage in such conduct. C and D are incorrect answers because the attorney will not be subject to discipline for the defendant's failure to appear when the attorney advised the defendant to appear as required and the defendant did not follow that advice.

QUESTION #44

B is the correct answer. MRPC 1.8(h)(2) prohibits attorneys from settling potential malpractice claims with an unrepresented client unless the client is advised in writing to seek independent legal counsel before making the agreement, and is given reasonable time to do so. Here, the facts show that the lawyer failed to take those required steps before formation of his agreement with the client. Thus, A is an incorrect answer. C is not a correct answer because, although factually accurate, the client might not have voluntarily entered into the agreement with the lawyer if the lawyer had properly advised the client to seek independent legal counsel and had provided enough time for the client to do that. D is a wrong answer because the lawyer did not engage in proper conduct when the lawyer admittedly failed to include a provision about refreshments in the contract with the company.

QUESTION #45

C is the correct answer. MRPC 1.11, which governs conduct for attorneys transitioning between government employment and private practice, prohibits a former public officer or government employee from representing a client in connection with a matter in which the attorney "participated personally and substantially" while employed by the government. The Rule provides an exception, however, if the government gives written consent. Additionally, if an attorney is disqualified by reason of her participation, then the new firm is also disqualified unless the attorney is screened in a timely manner and the agency is given notice of the screening to ascertain compliance with the rule. Here, the firm and the lawyer can remain involved in the representation because the attorney was promptly screened from the representation, such that the department can ensure compliance with MRPC 1.6, the Rule concerning confidentiality.

B is incorrect because, although factually accurate, MRPC 1.11's prohibition is not absolute, as C indicates and is explained above. For the same reasons, A is an incorrect answer because it broadly states the controlling Rule's effect without considering other facts referenced in the correct answer. D is a wrong answer because it describes a different Rule that does not apply here after the attorney ceased working for the department.

QUESTION #46

C is the correct answer because the attorney did not comply with MRPC 7.2. This Rule concerns information about legal services contained within advertising by attorneys. One of the Rule's comments provides that an attorney's advertisement may state the name of a regularly represented client, only with the client's consent. Here, the attorney regularly represents the client, Beta, pursuant to their contract. However, the attorney did not even inform the client of the brochure. Thus, the attorney lacks the client's consent to name the client in the brochure. Thus, she violated the Rule by stating in the advertisement that she represents the client. Accordingly, the attorney will be subject to discipline.

MRPC 7.2(c) requires that an attorney's advertisement, which communicates information about the attorney's services, must state the name and address of the attorney responsible for the advertisement. Here, the attorney complied with these requirements.

MRPC 7.4(a) permits an attorney to communicate the fact that the attorney practices particular types of law. Answers A, B, and D are not correct because the attorney identified the client without consent.

QUESTION #47

This is a very difficult question. B is the correct answer because the judge's personal policy is not fair to either party because the only grounds for granting a second continuance are either the death of, or a life-threatening physical condition of, a party or the party's counsel. The MCJC R 2.2 requires the judge to dispose of all judicial matters fairly. The judge's personal policy is not fair because of its extreme limitation on when the judge can grant a second continuance. A is a wrong answer because the facts state, and the call of the question indicates, that the judge is following his personal policy, not any legal requirement limiting the granting of a second continuance, and the law specifies that the granting of a continuance is at the judge's discretion. C is an incorrect answer because, as a result of the judge's personal policy, he has limited the scope of his discretion. Although it is factually accurate, D is a wrong answer because whether a party whose motion is denied can appeal is not the dispositive issue.

QUESTION #48

D is the correct answer because the attorney improperly utilized the client's funds. MRPC 1.15 requires attorneys to keep client funds separate from their own funds and to use client funds only to pay client expenses. Here, the attorney commingled personal and client funds and used client funds to pay his own personal expenses. Although factually accurate, C is a wrong answer because the fact that the client was assessed a penalty is less dispositive than the fact that the attorney utilized the client's funds. A is a wrong answer because the attorney's payments using the client's funds adversely affected the client because she was assessed a penalty. It is irrelevant that the attorney thought that the client would not object to those payments. B is an incorrect answer because, even if the client implicitly ratified the payments that the attorney made, that does not preclude the attorney from being subject to discipline for violating the controlling Rule.

QUESTION #49

A is the correct answer in this concurrent conflict of interest situation. A lawyer cannot generally represent two clients who have a concurrent conflict of interest. MRPC 1.7 states that a "concurrent conflict of interest exists if (1) the representation of one client will be directly adverse to another client; or (2) there is a significant risk that the representation of one or more clients will be materially limited by the lawyer's responsibilities to another client, a former client or a third person or by a personal interest of the lawyer." The litigation attorney's representation of the domestic headlight retailer would be improper because she is already currently representing the retailer, and the domestic headlight retailer's action is directly adverse to the interests of the retailer. There is an exception to this Rule prohibiting representation of clients with a concurrent conflict of interest, but it can only apply if the lawyer reasonably believes that the lawyer will be able to provide competent and diligent representation to each client. Because the domestic headlight retailer is challenging the retailer's application, the litigation attorney can have no such reasonable belief. B is a wrong answer because whether the tort lawsuit and the application to transact business case could be decided by the same appellate court is not the dispositive consideration as to whether the litigation attorney can properly represent the domestic headlight retailer. C is an incorrect answer because whether either the application to transact business or the tort action involves the same factual and legal issues is not the dispositive consideration as to whether the litigation attorney can properly represent the domestic headlight retailer because the action is still directly adverse. D is an incorrect answer because the distinction between the application to transact business being an administrative matter and the tort action being a civil action is not the dispositive consideration as to whether the litigation attorney can properly represent the domestic headlight retailer.

QUESTION #50

A is the correct answer because the Rules allow advertisements unless they are false or misleading. B is a wrong answer, although it raises a valid issue that if the advertisement is broadcast in other jurisdictions where the attorney is not licensed, the Rule against the unauthorized practice of law could apply. C is an incorrect answer because the Rules do not require that advertisements state a lawyer's credentials. D is a wrong answer because the attorney's advertisement is intended to offer legal services to people, rather than promote more lawsuits.

QUESTION #51

A is the correct answer because MRPC 1.8(d) prohibits an attorney from, before the conclusion of representation of a client, negotiating or making an agreement with the client giving the attorney literary or media rights to an account or portrayal based in substantial part on information regarding the representation. Here, the attorney is trying to make such an agreement before the conclusion of representation of the client by means of the provision that would improperly grant the rights to the attorney upon accepting representation. The attorney would make such an improper agreement if he and the client signed it upon the start of representation.

However, the attorney may not make such an agreement until *after* the attorney finishes representation of the client.

B is not correct because it states a blanket prohibition upon an agreement granting any right to an attorney upon accepting representation of a client. That categorical prohibition goes far beyond the scope of MRPC 1.8(d). As a practical matter, that prohibition could conflict with an attorney's ability to enter into such contracts granting rights, provided that they are lawful and do not violate the Rules.

C is a wrong answer because the law does not grant an attorney the right to publish a book about her client's case, and MRPC 1.8(d) governs this matter. D is incorrect because an attorney's discretion in contracting with clients is subject to the Rules and the law.

Incidentally, in order for the attorney to facilitate her clients' payment of her bills for legal fees, the attorney could: 1) enable clients to get loans from creditors with which to pay the legal fees; or 2) process payment of the legal fees by debit and credit cards along with checks.

QUESTION #52

A is the correct answer because it accurately applies the controlling Rule to the facts. MRPC 1.15 requires that an attorney withdraw funds from a client's trust account as they are earned, and may only place his personal funds in the client's trust account for the purpose of paying bank service charges. By failing to withdraw funds from the client trust account when earned, the attorney's funds became commingled with the client trust account's funds. B is a wrong answer because, although factually accurate, the attorney failed to properly withdraw his earnings from the client's funds as the earnings accrued. Although the attorney did not engage in improper conduct by receiving the client's payment in advance, the attorney engaged in improper conduct by not withdrawing funds upon earning them. C and D are incorrect answers because, although the attorney's placement of the funds in the account and regular issuance of invoices complied with the Rules to some extent, this compliance did not obviate the attorney from the obligation to withdraw the funds from the client trust account as earnings accrued. A provides the best answer because it addresses this improper handling of the funds by the attorney when the other answers refer to his proper handling of them.

QUESTION #53

C is the correct answer because the attorney can represent the estate even though he is likely to be a necessary witness because the attorney's testimony would relate to the uncontested issue of the deed's execution. MRPC 3.7(a) provides that an attorney may serve as an advocate and a necessary witness who testifies in the same trial if "(1) the testimony relates to an uncontested issue; (2) the testimony relates to the nature and value of legal services rendered in the case; or (3) disqualification of the" attorney would result in substantial hardship to the client. If the testimony, however, would have concerned a contested issue such as the deed's defective title, then the attorney could not represent the estate pursuant to MRPC 3.7(a)(1). Although it is factually accurate, D is an incorrect answer because the attorney's lack of a beneficial interest pursuant to the deed is not one of the exceptions to the Rule's prohibition on an attorney serving as both an advocate and a necessary witness in the same trial. A is a wrong answer because it refers to another exception to MRPC 3.7 that is not applicable under these facts. The facts do not indicate that the disqualification of the attorney would work a substantial hardship to the estate. B is an incorrect answer because the fact that the lawyer will call the attorney as a witness in the lawsuit does not automatically and completely prohibit the attorney from representing the estate.

QUESTION #54

B is the correct answer because it accurately reflects that, as required by the Rules, the client consented to the attorney's to association with the bankruptcy lawyer after the attorney explained it to the client. MRPC 1.1 requires a lawyer to provide competent representation to all clients. The comment to that rule states that "[c]ompetent representation can also be provided through the association of a lawyer of established competence in the field in question." In order to associate with another lawyer, though, an attorney would have to reveal confidential information to the lawyer, which, according to MRPC 1.6(a), requires the client's informed consent. A is a wrong answer because, as addressed earlier, the Rules regulate the attorney's association with the bankruptcy lawyer. C and D are incorrect answers because the attorney and the bankruptcy lawyer can associate under certain circumstances, such as here, when the client consents to the association after receiving information about it (even if they know each other personally).

QUESTION #55

C is the correct answer because MRPC 7.5(d) provides that members of the bar can only state or imply that they practice law as partners if that is true. Here, the replacement sign indicates that the attorney, the lawyer, and the counselor are practicing law in a partnership, and the facts do not support that representation. A is a wrong answer because a partnership does not result from them equally paying the costs of a secretary, paralegal, and answering service. D is an incorrect answer because members of the bar can refer to themselves as law partners if they are in fact members of the same partnership in a law firm. B is a wrong answer because the fact that the attorney, the lawyer, and the counselor refer prospective clients to each other does not make them law partners.

QUESTION #56

C is the correct answer because comment 2 of MCJC R 1.3 allows the judge to provide the letter because she knows the daughter and the facts do not indicate that the judge violated any Rule. Rather, the facts state that the letter contains only truthful statements, which are permissible. The judge did not write the letter for an improper purpose that would subject her for discipline for violating the controlling Rule, such as using her position to get special treatment or gain some personal advantage. Accordingly, D is wrong because no facts indicate that the letter will afford the judge an improper advantage when it could benefit the daughter and is not addressed to any particular recipient. B is an incorrect answer because, as mentioned earlier, the fact that the judge knows the daughter provides a reason why the judge will not be subject to discipline for providing the letter of recommendation. The fact that the judge is friends with the daughter's parents implicitly tends to support the fact that the judge personally knows the daughter.

A is not a correct answer because the fact that the judge wrote the letter on court stationary does not violate the Rule unless the judge had used her official letterhead in order to get some advantage in her personal business affairs. Here, the judge used such paper to write the letter for the daughter's benefit, not her own.

QUESTION #57

C is the correct answer because the attorney faced an emergency situation making it impractical to refer the matter to, or associate with, another lawyer in order to draft the will. The comment to MRPC 1.1 states that in an emergency situation where it would be impractical to consult with or refer a case to another lawyer, an attorney may give legal advice or assistance even when the attorney is not competent in the matter at issue. On the next day after becoming aware of the case, the attorney unsuccessfully attempted to refer the case to another lawyer. Given the nature of the situation, it would have been prudent for her to draft the will before the step-uncle's imminent decease. D is a wrong answer because a familial relationship is not an exception to the requirement of competence in a lawyer's representation of a client. Although factually accurate, both A and B are incorrect because their descriptions of the requirement of competence in representation are subject to the emergency exception that applies here.

QUESTION #58

B is the correct answer because the judge is not required to disqualify herself. Thus, her presiding over the case does not subject her to discipline for violating any rule. MCJC R 2.11 requires disqualification in a proceeding in which the judge's impartiality might reasonably be questioned. Here, the corporation may not reasonably question the judge's impartiality in the case based on the facts that she is one of five trustees of a trust that holds one millionth of its value in the company's stock. Under MCJC R 2.11(A)(3) a judge's impartiality might be reasonably be questioned, such that the judge must disqualify herself, when the judge knows that she, as a fiduciary, has an economic interest in the subject matter in dispute or a party to a proceeding before the judge. As the trust's trustee, the judge occupies a fiduciary position. Generally, an economic interest means ownership of more than a *de minimus* interest.

Here, the judge does not have to disqualify herself because she knows that, as a fiduciary of the trust, she does not have more than a *de minimus* interest in the case or the company. Moreover, the judge knows that, as a fiduciary, her economic interest in the case or the company is *de minimus* because the trust only contains one millionth of its value in the company's stock.

Accordingly, A is a wrong answer because, although factually accurate, even if the company stock ownership were attributed to her personally rather than as the trustee, she would still hold such a minimal interest as to not affect her impartiality. Therefore, C is an incorrect answer because it is likely that the judge could impartially handle the case. D is a wrong answer because the results of the case could impact the company stock's cost.

QUESTION #59

A is the correct answer because MRPC 5.6(b) prohibits the provision of this offer of compromise that restricts the attorney's right to practice law. Specifically, an attorney may not participate in offering or making an agreement in which a limitation on the attorney's "right to practice is part of the settlement of a client controversy." If this offer lacked the aforementioned type of prohibited provision, then it would not violate this Rule and would be a valid means of settling the case. C is a wrong answer because the Rule prohibits any restriction on the attorney's right to practice law, regardless of how minimal the impact of the restriction might be. B is an incorrect answer because the Rule does not provide an exception for the fact that another lawyer could provide the landowner competent representation in any other legal matter involving the neighbor. D is a wrong answer because the Rule is not conditional upon, and lacks an exception for, when an attorney believes that a settlement that limits the attorney's right to practice is the best method for a client to achieve its objectives, or is in the client's best interest.

QUESTION #60

D is the correct answer because, although the attorney can make a contribution to the lawyer's reelection committee, the attorney may not accept the appointment because he made the contribution for the purpose of obtaining or being considered for the appointment. Thus, A is not a correct answer because it makes an inaccurate statement that is too categorical.

B and C are incorrect answers because the propriety of the attorney's acceptance of the appointment is not contingent upon his established professional and financial relationship with the lawyer. Subject to certain limitations, MCJC R 3.11(A) permits the lawyer as a judge to hold and manage investments such as real estate.

QUESTION #61

C is the correct answer because, by telling the defendant why they cannot talk, the prosecutor complied with MRPC 4.2. Generally, this Rule prohibits the prosecutor from talking with the defendant because the attorney represents the defendant. The Rule applies even when the attorney is not present or the defendant tries to initiate the discussion. Thus, the prosecutor cannot speak with the defendant without the attorney being present. Pursuant to the Rule, the prosecutor immediately terminated the conversation that the defendant attempted to initiate. Therefore, A is wrong because prosecutor limited the communication with the defendant to only ending the defendant's attempted conversation. B is incorrect because the prosecutor complied with the Rule by presenting the plea agreement proposals to the attorney, rather than the defendant.

In the factual context of this question, the prosecutor would be subject to discipline for violating the Rule by replying to the defendant's statement with either of the following statements: 1) "That is an interesting development that we should discuss further." or 2) "I will consider doing that and let you know when my decision is made." By making either of these statements, the prosecutor would be speaking to the defendant in furtherance of the defendant's attempt to negotiate with the prosecutor directly, instead of through his attorney, when the prosecutor knows that the attorney represents the defendant. In that event, the prosecutor would be subject to discipline.

D is not a correct answer because: 1) the prosecutor has no need for immunity from discipline for what occurred here; and 2) immunity does not exist for what could have occurred here in violation of the Rule. Federal constitutional law may provide the President of the United States with absolute immunity for civil actions seeking money damages arising from the President's conduct while in office. Although the prosecutor represents an executive branch, it is part of the state's government. For those reasons, that legal principle does not apply here.

QUESTION #62

A is the correct answer because MRPC 3.9 requires the attorney to disclose that he appeared before the committee as the company's representative. B is a wrong answer because the company's payment to the attorney for testifying did not violate the Rule. C is an incorrect answer because the duty of client-lawyer confidentiality does not apply when the Rule required the attorney to reveal his relationship with the company. D is a wrong answer because the attorney-client evidentiary privilege does not apply when the Rule required the attorney to reveal his relationship with the company.

QUESTION #63

D is the correct answer because in this emergency situation the scope of the attorney's representation of the friend is limited to what is reasonably necessary under the circumstances. Generally, MRPC 1.1 requires that an attorney provide competent representation to clients. But in an emergency situation, when the attorney cannot reasonably consult with or refer a case to another, more competent lawyer, she may give advice or assistance. Even in this situation, though, the advice or assistance is limited to what is reasonably necessary given the circumstances. A is a wrong answer because the fact that the attorney assisted the friend because of their relationship does not make the attorney's conduct improper. B is an incorrect answer because, although the attorney lacked the requisite legal competence to handle the friend's matter, in this situation it was proper for her to assist the friend. C is not a correct answer because the fact that the attorney attempted to obtain the boy's release from the police station does not make the attorney's conduct proper.

QUESTION #64

C is the correct answer because, prior to the civil pretrial conference, the attorney obtained the plaintiff's informed consent to go to trial during the summer. MRPC 1.4 requires an attorney to keep his client reasonably informed about the status of the case and explain situations arising during representation so that the client may make informed decisions. Here, the attorney timely informed the plaintiff of the trial date, and correctly counseled her that it would not negatively affect her interests. A is a wrong answer because the attorney acted appropriately. B is an incorrect answer because it is not relevant when the facts do not indicate a speedy trial issue. Even if D describes a valid general principle, it is a wrong answer because that principle is not the dispositive consideration for answering this question

QUESTION #65

C is the correct answer because the attorney improperly made a false statement of material fact to a third party, which MRPC 4.1(a) prohibits in the course of representation. This false statement is that the battery operated "the longest before recharge of any battery ever produced." The attorney said this despite the inventor's prior statement to the contrary. This third factor about the invention's novelty could have been decisive in either the lawyer's or the manufacturer's decision-making process regarding whether to agree to license the invention. Accordingly, D is a wrong answer because the attorney did not simply "overstate" the invention's capabilities. A is an incorrect answer because the attorney's statement violated the Rule, whether he made his statement to the lawyer, the manufacturer, or any other third party. B is a wrong answer because the attorney's description of the invention did not merely constitute harmless "puffing" for sales purposes.

QUESTION #66

C is the correct answer because the attorney violated MRPC 1.2(d), which prohibits him from assisting the defendant in conduct that the attorney knows is criminal. Moreover, attorneys may not counsel clients to engage in conduct that the attorney knows is criminal or fraudulent. While the Rule permits attorneys to discuss the legal consequences of a course of action, here the attorney overstepped that limit. The attorney's statement to the defendant that he could avoid trial by going back to the country, and any research necessary to make that statement accurate, assisted the defendant in breaking the law in terms of disobeying the terms of his pretrial release and applicable laws against fleeing and eluding the police. D is a wrong answer because it is implicitly contained within the more dispositive answer C. Although factually correct, A and B are incorrect answers because the Rule lacks exceptions applicable in those circumstances.

QUESTION #67

B is the correct answer because in this situation the judge's disqualification is mandatory and a proper waiver of disqualification did not occur. Under MCJC R 2.11(A), a judge is required to disqualify herself from a proceeding in which her impartiality might reasonably be questioned. Under MCJC R 2.11(A)(2), a judge's impartiality might be reasonably questioned, such that the judge must disqualify herself, when she knows that she or her spouse has more than a *de minimis* economic interest that could be substantially affected by the proceeding. This provision applies because the husband owns a significant quantity of the large corporation's stock. However, MCJC R 2.11(C) allows the parties and attorneys to waive disqualification if the judge discloses the basis of her disqualification and asks the parties and their attorneys to consider waiving disqualification. If they agree, without the judge's participation, that the judge should not be disqualified, then she may participate in the proceeding. Answer B reflects that the waiver did not conform to the Rule's requirement that the agreement of the parties and their attorneys to waive disqualification occur without the judge's participation. A is a wrong answer because it inaccurately indicates that the Rules do not provide for waiver of disqualification, which can occur under certain circumstances. Although it is factually accurate, C is an incorrect answer because the disqualification that must occur here is not subject to an exception on the basis that a judge is particularly well prepared to preside over the case. D is wrong because, even if the judge would be impartial notwithstanding the husband's ownership of large corporation stock, that is not an exception to the disqualification requirement.

QUESTION #68

D is the correct answer because the commercial does not include the information required by MRPC 7.2. Specifically, subject to other requirements within the Rules, an attorney may advertise his services through public media, but any advertisement must include the attorney's name and office address. However, the attorney's commercial complies with all of the other requirements, including that the advertisement not be false or misleading with regard to his services. MRPC 7.1. A, then, is incorrect because the advertisement does not comply with all of the Rules' requirements. C is a wrong answer because the commercial need not indicate whether a fee will be charged for the initial consultation. B is an incorrect answer because the Rules do not require or prohibit the use of a professional to record a commercial.

QUESTION #69

C is correct because the attorney did not handle the check as required by MRPC 1.15(d). Pursuant to that Rule, the attorney should have processed the check by depositing it in a client trust account for the plaintiff, notifying the plaintiff of its receipt, and mailing the plaintiff a $75,000 check issued from the client trust account.

The attorney did not follow that proper approach by endorsing the defendant's check and forwarding it to the plaintiff. Alternatively, note that the attorney would have followed an improper approach by depositing the defendant's check in the attorney's general account for the plaintiff, notifying the plaintiff of its receipt, and mailing the plaintiff a $75,000 check issued from the general account. In that event, the attorney would have used the wrong type of account, rather than a proper, client trust account.

Because the attorney improperly processed the check in violation of the Rule, A, B, and D are not correct because their factually accurate reasons all lead to wrong conclusions.

QUESTION #70

C is the correct answer because the dispositive issue is competent representation, not whether the defendant provides informed consent to the attorney's continued sole representation. Thus, B is an incorrect answer because, although based on informed consent, the defendant's decision to accept the attorney's continued sole representation does not relieve the attorney of the duty to provide competent representation.

MRPC 1.1 requires an attorney to provide competent representation to clients. In order to do that, the attorney may need to learn enough to become competent or associate with an attorney having competence. D is the wrong answer because the attorney does not have to be or become a certified specialist in criminal defense in order to satisfy the Rule's requirement of competence.

A is wrong because the attorney's representation of the defendant is not automatically or necessarily proper simply because the trial judge appointed her as sole counsel. Again, the attorney's competence is a key prerequisite to proper representation.

In response to her realization, the attorney could have taken a couple of steps to properly address the competence requirement. The attorney could have informed the judge that she lacks the legal competence to try the case and wants to make a permissive withdrawal from being the defendant's counsel. Alternatively, the attorney could have informed the judge that he needs to appoint a co-counsel with legal competence in this subject matter and grant a postponement of the trial in order for both defense counsels to properly prepare for it.

QUESTION #71

C is the correct answer because the creditor and the plaintiff both claim interests in the damages recovered, which are disputed property. MRPC 1.15(e) requires an attorney to keep disputed property received by him separate until the dispute is resolved when two or more people claim an interest in that property. The attorney must immediately distribute any portion of that property that is not in dispute. The comment to MRPC 1.15(e) provides that applicable law can obligate the attorney to protect a third-party's lawful claims upon a client's funds, which the lawyer possesses, from a client's wrongful interference. In that event, if the third-party's claim is not frivolous, the lawyer may not release the funds or property to the client until resolution of the competing claims occurs. The facts state that applicable law provides that the creditor has a lawful claim, which the attorney has a legal duty to protect, and that the claim is not frivolous.

Thus, the attorney may not disburse the disputed $2,400 until resolution of the dispute occurs. However, the attorney must promptly disburse the other $12,600 to the client.

Accordingly, A is a wrong answer because, although the plaintiff recovered the damages, a portion of them is subject to the creditor's claim of lien and in dispute. B is an incorrect answer because it is factually inaccurate when the facts indicate that the creditor is entitled to some of those funds. D is a wrong answer because the fact that the attorney informed the plaintiff that the creditor would enforce its legal rights against the plaintiff does not subject the attorney to discipline because the attorney has a duty to communicate with the plaintiff.

QUESTION #72

C is the correct answer because MRPC 1.8 only permits an aggregate settlement based on each of the homeowner's informed written consent if they are also informed about every other homeowner's participation in the settlement. Comment 13 to the Rule contemplates that an attorney must inform all clients in an aggregate group of the material terms of the settlement including the amounts awarded to each client. Here, the attorney did not inform each of the homeowners about every other homeowner's participation in the settlement in terms of their respective settlement amounts. Accordingly, A is a wrong answer because the Rule requires the attorney to reveal all settlement amounts, even if doing that could undermine the prospects of the offer's universal acceptance. B is an incorrect answer because the attorney will not have fully complied with the Rule simply because each of the homeowners will receive a fair settlement amount and each of them will accept it. D is a wrong answer because it inaccurately reflects the above described Rule.

QUESTION #73

D is the correct answer because MRPC 3.4 prohibits an attorney from unlawfully obstructing another party's access to evidence or conceal something with potential evidentiary value. Here, the lawyer violated the Rule by neither providing the note nor referring to it at all, when the lawyer did not have any lawful basis for preventing the plaintiff's discovery of the note. Generally, the attorney may discover any evidence that is relevant to the controversy, provided that the evidence is neither privileged nor work product. Here, the lawyer cannot contend that the law of either attorney-client privilege nor work product protection make lawful his obstruction of the attorney's access to the note and concealment of it. Thus, answers A and B are not correct. C is an incorrect answer because the lawyer does not have any constitutional duty to disclose the note as would a prosecutor have a duty to disclose exculpatory evidence to a criminal defendant. However, the Rule prohibits the lawyer's unlawful obstruction of the attorney's access to the note and his concealment of it.

QUESTION #74

C is the correct answer because the attorney cannot represent the patient after having represented the organization because doing so would involve a conflict of interest. As a general rule, MPRC 1.9(b) prohibits a lawyer from knowingly representing "a person in the same or a substantially related manner in which a firm with which the lawyer formerly was associated had previously represented a client (1) whose interests are material adverse to that person; and (2) about whom the lawyer had acquired [confidential information] that is material to the matter." The organization qualifies as a type of law firm.

Here, the attorney worked for the organization and represented it in all of its legal dealings, including the matter giving rise to the patient's proposed lawsuit. The attorney was privy to confidential information pertinent to the patient's application, so unless the organization gives informed, written consent to this proposed representation pursuant to MPRC 1.9(a), the attorney may not represent the patient. Therefore, answer B is incorrect because, even though the attorney no longer represents the organization, representing the patient would violate the Rule unless the organization provides informed consent. As a practical matter, that is not likely to occur.

Note that the attorney may not permit another member of the firm to assist the patient without the attorney receiving any share of the fee in that matter. Under MRPC 1.10(a), that situation would also involve an improper conflict of interest, which would be imputed to the firm's other members.

A is a wrong answer because, although factually accurate regarding the attorney's apparent competence to handle the patient's case, the Rule against conflicts of interest controls this situation and trumps application of the Rule regarding competence.

Answer D is not correct because the amount of time that the attorney has worked at the law firm is not a relevant factor relating to the rule against conflict of interest. In other words, the rule lacks any factor that takes into account how much time has passed between when the attorney represented one client whose interests conflict with the attorney's other, prospective client.

In this situation, the attorney could provide the patient with a list of recommended lawyers who are qualified to assist him, or decline to speak with the patient about the proposed lawsuit.

QUESTION #75

A is the correct answer because it is most related to MRPC 1.9 as it applies here regarding conflicts of interest. Generally, a lawyer may not knowingly represent "a person in the same or a substantially related manner in which a firm with which the lawyer formerly was associated had previously represented a client (1) whose interests are material adverse to that person; and (2) about whom the lawyer had acquired [confidential information] that is material to the matter." The company qualifies as a type of law firm.

Here, the Rule does prohibit the attorney from representing the individual, a new client, because this representation against the company, a former client, would not involve the same or substantially related matter as the one in which he previously represented the company. A tort lawsuit is the subject matter of the attorney's new representation of the individual against the company. An unrelated insurance claim was the subject matter of the attorney's former representation of the company in relation to the individual. These two separate matters are neither identical nor substantially related, such that it is proper for the attorney to represent the individual.

B is not a correct answer because it is less related to MRPC 1.9 than answer A is, when the fact that the attorney no longer represents the company does not necessarily mean that the attorney's later representation of the individual would be proper. Rather, answer A refers to the dispositive fact that the attorney's present representation of the individual would not concern the same or a substantially related manner as the attorney's former representation of the company. Accordingly, answer C is incorrect because the attorney may represent the individual now although he previously represented the company. Answer D is wrong because the fact that the attorney examined the individual's claim is not dispositive in light of the foregoing explanation.

QUESTION #76

A is the correct answer because MRPC 1.8(h) provides that an attorney may not make an agreement, such as the retainer contract and waiver form, that prospectively limits the attorney's exposure to legal malpractice liability to a client unless the client is independently represented by another lawyer when making the agreement. Although the attorney offered the client an opportunity to have another lawyer review the retainer contract and waiver form, the attorney made the offer after he gave them to her. Moreover, the client lacked independent representation when making the agreement. B is a wrong answer because the attorney may use the same form when representing most clients. C is an incorrect answer because the attorney violated the Rule, even though he provided consideration by agreeing to represent the client. D is a wrong answer because the attorney violated the Rule, regardless of whether he thinks that his hourly rate is reasonable and he is qualified to represent the client.

QUESTION #77

C is the correct answer because MRPC 7.2(b)(4) generally provides that an attorney cannot pay a non-lawyer professional such as the dealer for referrals except in certain situations. The arrangement here, however, does not qualify as one of those situations for two reasons. First, this reciprocal referral contract is exclusive, which MRPC 7.2(b)(4)(i) does not permit, because both the dealer and the attorney must only refer "any" of their respective customers or clients to each other. Second, the facts indicate that the attorney does not inform the clients of the contract's existence and nature, as required by MRPC 7.2(b)(4)(ii). A is a wrong answer because the contract here is not a fee sharing arrangement that is generally prohibited under another governing Rule. B is an incorrect answer because the contract is invalid because it improperly provides for referrals. B's issue of the reasonableness of the fees charged by the dealer and the attorney is not dispositive. D is a wrong answer because the contract does not provide for the attorney's practice of law with the dealer.

QUESTION #78

A is the correct answer for two reasons, despite the husband's directive that the lawyer must take an aggressive approach to litigation. First, the lawyer can exercise reasonable discretion in the conduct of litigation by agreeing to reschedule the deposition. MRPC 1.2 provides that a client determines the objectives of the representation, but the means of accomplishing those objectives is generally within an attorney's discretion. Second, the lawyer will not be subject to discipline because such an agreement would not prejudice the husband's rights. According to the first reason above, C is a wrong answer because the lawyer is not required to follow the husband's directive. Similarly, D is an incorrect answer because the lawyer did not need the husband's approval to reschedule the deposition. B is a wrong answer because, although the attorney has the right to determine the means of the representation, the client has the right to determine the objectives of the representation.

QUESTION #79

C is the correct answer because MRPC 1.15(b) allows an attorney to deposit the attorney's own funds in a client trust account for the sole purpose of paying bank service charges on that account, but only in an amount necessary for that purpose. Here, the attorney's conduct complied with the Rule. However, if the attorney had deposited more than was required to pay bank service charges, then the attorney would have made an improper deposit, which would make A correct. However, A is not correct because the attorney only deposited the amount necessary to pay the bank service charge. Thus, B is a wrong answer because the attorney could not improperly commingle his funds with the client's when the attorney followed the Rule. As a factual matter, B is an incorrect answer because the attorney's funds could not commingle with the client's funds because the client trust account had a zero balance. D is not correct because the fact that the client had a legal status of a missing person does not affect the Rule's application to these facts.

QUESTION #80

D is the correct answer. Ordinarily, MRPC 5.4(a) does not allow attorneys to share legal fees with non-lawyers, but there are exceptions to that general rule. The rule serves to protect an attorney's independent professional judgment. D is the correct answer for two reasons. First, the facts indicate that the staff cannot control the attorney's judgment because he supervises them and delegates work to them, which is subject to his review. Second, MRPC 5.4(a)(3) allows the attorney to include non-lawyer employees in his compensation plan, which is partially based on a profit-sharing arrangement. Accordingly, A is a wrong answer. B is an incorrect answer because the facts do not indicate that the staff is practicing law by doing secretarial, clerical, and paralegal work. Thus, the attorney is not improperly assisting them in unauthorized practice of law in violation of the Rules. C is a wrong answer because in the attorney's office his staff's access to client files may be necessary and unavoidable for purposes of performing their work.

QUESTION #81

C is the correct answer because MRPC 3.6(c) allows an attorney to make a statement that a reasonable attorney would consider necessary to protect a client from the substantial undue prejudicial effect of recent publicity not initiated by the attorney or the attorney's client. Here, the attorney reasonably considered his truthful statement necessary to protect the instructor from the substantial undue prejudicial effect of the prosecutor's press conference that neither the attorney nor the instructor initiated. That press conference appears to have had such an impact based on the media survey results showing that most people believed that the instructor is guilty. A is a wrong answer because the attorney complied with the Rule when he called and participated in the press conference. Likewise, B is an incorrect answer because the instructor permitted the attorney to call and hold the press conference, such that the instructor allowed the attorney to state information provided to him by the instructor.

D is not a correct answer because the fact that the instructor permitted the attorney to call and hold the press conference does not satisfy the above Rule's terms for when the attorney may make the statement that the attorney did. Although client consent is one exception to the Rule of confidentiality that seems satisfied by the instructor's permission, the question tests the main issue of whether the Rule allows the attorney to make the statement that he did.

The prosecutor might have violated MRPC 3.6(a) by making his extrajudicial statement about the instructor that he reasonably should have known would have been disseminated by means of a public communication and would have a substantial likelihood of materially prejudicing an adjudicative proceeding, i.e. a potential trial of the instructor, in the matter of the girl's accusation.

QUESTION #82

C is the correct answer because it would be improper for the judge to decide the case because one could reasonably question his impartiality about it. Generally, MCJC R 2.11(A)(2) requires a judge to disqualify himself in a proceeding in which the judge's impartiality might reasonably be questioned. Here, one could reasonably question the judge's impartiality in deciding the case on appeal after he directly participated in the department's prosecution of it at trial. Under MCJC R 2.11(A)(6)(b), a judge's impartiality might be reasonably be questioned, such that the judge must disqualify himself, when the judge served in governmental employment, and in this capacity participated substantially and personally as a public official or lawyer regarding the proceeding. Here, this provision requires disqualification of the judge from deciding the case on appeal because, while employed by the department, he worked substantially and personally as the state's attorney in the same case. Thus, B is a wrong answer because, although comparable to C, it does not refer to the controlling Rule as clearly as C does.

D is an incorrect answer because, although factually correct, the judge's lack of personal economic interest in the case does not affect his mandatory disqualification as explained earlier. However, note that mandatory disqualification can result when a judge has a sufficient economic interest in a case before the judge.

A is a wrong answer because the judge's disclosure of his role the case would be insufficient to make it proper for him to participate in deciding it. Moreover, the judge's failure to disclose his role in the case is not a basis for mandatory disqualification.

QUESTION #83

B is the correct answer. Generally, MCJC R 3.13(A) provides that a judge must not accept a gift if "acceptance is prohibited by law or would appear to a reasonable person to undermine the judge's independence, integrity, or impartiality." Here, the facts indicate that the judge's acceptance of the gift is neither prohibited by law nor otherwise unethical. Accordingly, A is an incorrect answer because the judge's acceptance of the sculpted bust as a gift, of itself, will not subject the judge to discipline.

MCJC R 3.13(C)(1) provides that, unless otherwise prohibited (which is not the case here as explained above), a judge may accept certain types of items, but must publicly report accepted "gifts incident to a public testimonial." Here, the judge received the bust as a gift from the state bar's committee pursuant to a public testimonial that occurred at the philanthropy's dinner. Accordingly, C is not a correct answer because that Rule allows for the judge's receipt of that gift incident to a public testimonial. In other words, of itself, that fact does not subject the judge to discipline. However, the judge failed to submit any regulatory paperwork about the gift as required by the foregoing Rule. Moreover, MCJC R 3.15(D) states that, generally, the judge must file such a report as a public document in the court on which the judge serves or another office designated by law. Thus, B is the correct answer because the judge failed to officially account for receiving the sculpted bust by not filing a public report about receiving it.

D is a wrong answer because the judge's uncompensated service on the board does not qualify as an exception or defense to application of the Rule requiring the judge to make a public report of receiving the sculpted bust as a gift.

QUESTION #84

The correct answer is D because, although the facts provide no reason to consider the agreement unlawful, its 100-year duration is not reasonable as a practical matter. Because the new partner and firm entered into an agreement of an unreasonable duration, they have violated MRPC 5.4(a)(1). Generally, this Rule provides that a law firm must not share legal fees with a non-attorney. However, one of the Rule's exceptions states in part that an agreement by an attorney with the attorney's firm may provide for the payment of money to the attorney's estate for a reasonable time period after the attorney's death. Here, the new partner made such an agreement with the firm. However, the agreement improperly obligates the firm make the payments for 100 years, which is not a reasonable duration. Thus, answer A is not correct because, although the agreement apparently is lawful, it is not ethical. Answer C is incorrect because the agreement apparently is lawful. Answer B is wrong because, as explained earlier, the applicable Rule limits agreements between the firm and its attorneys regarding the sharing or division of legal fees with a non-lawyer.

QUESTION #85

Answer B is correct because: 1) before the trial, the witness told the attorney that the defendant was in the state with her; and 2) at the trial, no evidence supported the attorney's statement that the defendant was in another state. MRPC 3.3(a)(1) provides that an attorney is prohibited from making a false statement of material fact or law to the court. Here, it is a material fact as to whether the defendant was in the state when the hunter was shot because the defendant could not have shot the hunter if the defendant was absent from the state then. The attorney made a false statement of material fact by saying that the defendant was out of the state when the witness had told the attorney otherwise and no evidence at trial supported the attorney's statement. Thus, the attorney improperly misled the court by stating as fact what the witness contradicted and the attorney knew lacked an evidentiary basis.

Answer A is wrong because, although factually correct, the attorney's false statement of material fact violated the Rule, not the fact that no evidence supported the statement. In other words, answer A states a reason why the attorney's statement was false, not that the false statement subjects the attorney to discipline. Answer C is not correct because the attorney's duty to zealously represent a client does not excuse the attorney from the duty to be truthful to the court. Answer D is incorrect because even assuming that the attorney used best efforts, that does not spare the attorney from discipline for making the false statement.

QUESTION #86

D is the correct answer because it accurately applies MRPC 1.6 to these facts. The Rule states that an attorney may not reveal confidential information provided by a client unless certain situations arise. Under MRPC 1.6(b)(1), one such situation exists when revealing the information will "prevent reasonably certain death or substantial bodily harm." Here, the attorney would prevent the victim's reasonably certain death by disclosing the victim's location to the police because the defendant's accomplice will kill the victim due to the state's refusal to pay the ransom. Thus, A is an incorrect answer because, although the defendant's statement is subject to the Rule, the Rule does not protect it from disclosure under these circumstances. C is not a correct answer because the admission of guilt is protected by client-lawyer confidentiality.

B is a wrong answer because the Rule (and its relevant exception) applies regardless of whether its application would conflict with the defendant's best interest.

QUESTION #87

D is the correct answer because MRPC 1.11(a)(2) generally prohibits the attorney's representation of the citizen following her personal and substantial involvement in the city's action against the citizen. In order to undertake such representation, the attorney must obtain the former client's informed written consent. C is a wrong answer because the Rule's exception requires written rather than oral consent. Thus, the exception could apply if the attorney had obtained the city's informed consent, confirmed in writing, to representing the client. A is a wrong answer because merely ceasing to represent the city would not permit the attorney to accept representation against the city in a matter in which she substantially participated. B is an incorrect answer because, although the attorney can have clients while employed by the city, the Model Rules limits who she may represent. Here, the attorney did not comply with the Rule requiring the city's informed written consent prior to representing the citizen.

QUESTION #88

The correct answer is B because: 1) the attorney did not satisfy the requirement of MRPC 1.1, which imposes the duty of competence upon an attorney representing a client; and 2) pursuant to MRPC 5.2(a), the attorney had to comply with MRPC 1.1 when acting at the managing partner's direction. MRPC 5.2(a) provides that all of the Rules bind an attorney even when the attorney acted at another person's direction. Thus, an attorney may not escape responsibility for violating a Rule -- such as MRPC 1.1 here -- simply because the associate attorney acted at the other person's direction. Therefore, answer C incorrectly indicates that the associate attorney will not be subject to discipline because she acted at the managing partner's direction.

Generally, among other things, under the duty of competence the attorney must apply the diligence (i.e., thoroughness and preparation), learning, and skill reasonably necessary for the performance of the legal service requested. Here, the attorney did not act competently in her legal representation of the client because she did not sufficiently apply those attributes in order to find and comply with the provision requiring special service of process for the client's medical malpractice action.

A is not correct because it is not clear from the facts whether the associate attorney should have declined undertaking the case. Moreover, the associate attorney could have sought assistance from another more experienced attorney.

Answer D is wrong because, as addressed earlier, the associate attorney will be subject to disciplinary action regardless of the action's dollar value.

QUESTION #89

D is the correct answer because the attorney properly gave advice that included both legal and economic factors. MRPC 2.1 allows the attorney to refer to both the law and other non-legal considerations, "such as moral, economic, social and political factors." Thus, A is a wrong answer because the attorney complied with the Rule by providing advice including both legal and economic factors. B is an incorrect answer because the attorney's advice not to pursue the small claim complied with the Rule. The attorney should fulfill the duty of zealous advocacy of the sales company's interests subject to other controlling Rules. C is a wrong answer because the determination of whether the attorney engaged in proper conduct should not depend upon whether the president accepted the attorney's advice or not. That determination should depend upon whether the attorney complied with the Rule.

QUESTION #90

A is the correct answer. MRPC 3.3(a)(1) prohibits an attorney from knowingly making a false statement of fact. Here, the false statement of fact was that the evidence was undisputed about the traffic light's color when the accident occurred. Although the new lawyer did make a false statement of fact to the court, he was unaware of the statement's falsity. Once he becomes aware of the falsity, he is obligated to correct the error. Until then, however, he is not subject to discipline. Thus, C is incorrect because it does not address the fact that the new lawyer did not know of the falsity of the statement. Although factually accurate, B is a wrong answer because the new lawyer will be subject to discipline for a known misrepresentation even if it is not the first instance of the misrepresentation. D is an incorrect answer because this situation may qualify under the emergency exception to the competence Rule given the suddenness of the attorney's stroke and the time constraints on the new lawyer.

QUESTION #91

A is the correct answer because, although MRPC 8.3(a) imposes upon the attorney a general duty to report the lawyer's violation of the Rules that raises a substantial question as to the lawyer's honesty, trustworthiness, and fitness to act as an attorney, the criminal law attorney does not have to so when doing that would violate MRPC 1.6, which governs client-lawyer confidentiality. In other words, MRPC 8.3(c) and its second comment do not require a report of misconduct that would violate the Rule of confidentiality by disclosing information it protects. Here, the probate lawyer apparently violated the Rules by his misconduct under MPRC 8.4(b) of misusing his client funds, which arguably constitutes a crime that reflects adversely upon his honesty, trustworthiness, and fitness as an attorney. However, the probate lawyer disclosed that violation during the attorney's representation of him as a client. Generally, this prevents the criminal law attorney from disclosing the probate lawyer's statements to him. Usually, MRPC 1.6(a) provides that an criminal law attorney may not reveal confidential information without informed consent or because he must do so to represent the client. The facts do not support application of either of these grounds for the attorney to reveal confidential information about the probate lawyer. The Rule provides several exceptions, one of which allows an attorney to reveal confidential information in order to prevent substantial injury to the financial interests of a third party, but only when the client is using the attorney's services in furtherance of the actions causing the injury. MRPC 1.6(b)(2)-(3). Here, although the probate lawyer's clients may have sustained injury to their financial interests due to his misuse of their funds, the facts do not indicate that the probate lawyer is now using the criminal law attorney's services in order to do that. Rather, the criminal law attorney advised the probate lawyer not to do that again and directed him to obtain assistance with his gambling addiction. Note that MRPC 8.3(c) does not require the criminal law attorney to disclose information that he obtained from the probate lawyer while the criminal law attorney is participating in the lawyer assistance program. Arguably, this could apply because the criminal law attorney served on the state bar committee that oversees the assistance program when the probate lawyer retained him.

B is a wrong answer because, although it relates to a provision of MRPC 8.3 governing reporting professional misconduct, the facts do not indicate that any lawyer in the probate lawyer's law firm has knowledge of the probate lawyer's misconduct. C is a wrong answer because the criminal law attorney's duty of confidentiality to the lawyer existed once the probate lawyer made his statement to the attorney. D is an incorrect answer because the criminal law attorney's duty of confidentiality trumps the concern that he will help conceal the probate lawyer's breach of fiduciary duty.

QUESTION #92

A is the correct answer in this *ex parte* communication situation. MCJC R 2.9(A) provides that, subject to certain exceptions, a judge must not initiate, permit, or consider *ex parte* communications, or consider other communications made to the judge outside the presence of the parties, regarding an impending or pending matter. MCJC R 2.9(A)(2) provides one exception that applies to the advice of a disinterested expert on the law applicable to a case before a judge. The judge is permitted to obtain the written advice of a disinterested expert if she gives the parties notice and sufficient time to respond. Here, the exception does not apply because, even assuming that the attorney qualifies as a disinterested expert on the law, the judge did not obtain written advice from the attorney. Moreover, the judge did not provide the parties with any notice or time to respond. Thus, the judge permitted and considered improper communications with the attorney about the case outside the parties' presence. B is an incorrect answer because a judge can obtain the opinion of a disinterested third party expert under the circumstances described above. D is a wrong answer because, although the attorney may have been disinterested in terms of not representing a client involved in the case, it was not proper for the judge to consult with the attorney in this situation. C is an incorrect answer because the fact that attorney called the judge and the judge did not call the attorney is irrelevant.

QUESTION #93

C is the correct answer because it reflects MRPC 5.4(b), which prohibits the attorney from forming a partnership with a non-lawyer that involves any activities of practicing law. D is a wrong answer because the dispositive issue is whether the attorney formed a partnership that involves his practice of law in this relationship with the physician, a non-lawyer. C directly involves that issue and implicates the controlling Rule. D indirectly involves that issue and implicates the Rule, which the attorney would violate as a result of practicing law in a partnership formed with the physician, a non-lawyer. If the attorney did not practice law in their partnership, then there would be no legal fees to possibly divide or share. In addition, implicitly D refers to this issue of fee-sharing among the attorney and the physician, a non-lawyer. MRPC 5.4(a) prohibits the attorney from sharing legal fees with a non-lawyer such as the physician. Although it may be factually accurate, A is an incorrect answer because the relationship of the attorney and the physician will violate MRPC 5.4(b). B is a wrong answer because a violation of MRPC 5.4(b) would occur even if the physician did not provide clients with legal advice.

QUESTION #94

C is the correct answer because it is the best option. MRPC 8.4 provides that an attorney commits misconduct by engaging in behavior that involves dishonesty, fraud, deceit, or misrepresentation. Under MRPC 8.3, an attorney who knows of another attorney's violation of the Rules that raises questions regarding the other attorney's honesty, trustworthiness, and fitness to act as an attorney, must report such behavior.

Answer C refers to evidence that the prosecutor has that arguably could support him in reporting his concerns about the attorney's motive. Such evidence could show that the attorney engaged in misconduct under MRPC 8.4, such that the prosecutor must report that misconduct pursuant to MRPC 8.3. Primarily, this evidence consists of what the prosecutor heard the attorney say to his friend about recommending rejection of the offer to the defendant. Additionally, the facts contain other circumstantial evidence including the defendant's rejection of the offer, and the media coverage of the trial. Arguably, further evidence could exist if the attorney's recommendation misled the defendant, or included any other false or untruthful statements. Although the attorney's recommendation truthfully states what could happen, the prosecutor has a reasonable belief about the attorney's improper motive based on the circumstantial evidence and rather unlikely possibility of acquittal at the trial. Moreover, the attorney might have misled, or not been truthful toward, the defendant by: 1) not qualifying the likelihood of an acquittal; and 2) not explaining the likelihood of a conviction in light of the facts. The latter possibility is significant because conviction of a capital crime may result in the death penalty. The defendant could have avoided that result by accepting the offer, and might have wanted to do so if the attorney had more fully advised him about these scenarios. The attorney should have done that in the defendant's best interest.

A is a wrong answer because if the attorney violated the Rule, the prosecutor would still have to report the attorney despite his providing the defendant with effective assistance of counsel at the trial. B is an incorrect answer because the fact that a defendant could get an acquittal as a result of a trial, which he could not have received by accepting the offer, does not necessarily indicate that the attorney violated the Rule. Rather, it could show that the attorney's motive for recommending that the defendant reject the offer was to seek an acquittal. D is a wrong answer because, although the trial of the case received media coverage, that does not necessarily indicate that the attorney violated the Rule.

QUESTION #95

A is the correct answer because the attorney may be subject to civil liability because the paralegal negligently failed to make an entry in her case calendar while working for the attorney on the client's case. The civil liability may come in the form of vicarious liability, which the attorney would be liable for even if the attorney was not negligent. A is also correct because the attorney could be in violation of MRPC 5.3(b)-(c), and thus subject to discipline, if he failed to properly supervise the paralegal. B is a wrong answer because it incorrectly states that the attorney will avoid either discipline or civil liability based on his lack of negligence, when the attorney may have civil liability for the paralegal's negligence pursuant to the doctrine of vicarious liability. C is an incorrect answer because vicarious liability is not a basis for finding the attorney subject to both discipline and civil liability for the assistance's negligence, although it is a basis for finding the attorney subject to civil liability. D is a wrong answer because the client cannot make the decision of whether the attorney is subject to discipline or civil liability. The determination of whether the attorney is subject to discipline must be made by the jurisdiction's disciplinary authority. The determination of the attorney 's civil liability for the paralegal's negligence must be made by the relevant court of competent jurisdiction.

QUESTION #96

C is the correct answer because it reflects MRPC 5.4(b), which prohibits the attorney from forming a partnership with a non-lawyer that involves any activities of practicing law. D is a wrong answer because the dispositive issue is whether the attorney formed a partnership that involves his practice of law in this relationship with the physician, a non-lawyer. C directly involves that issue and implicates the controlling Rule. D indirectly involves that issue and implicates the Rule, which the attorney would violate as a result of practicing law in a partnership formed with the physician, a non-lawyer. If the attorney did not practice law in their partnership, then there would be no legal fees to possibly divide or share. In addition, implicitly D refers to this issue of fee-sharing among the attorney and the physician, a non-lawyer. MRPC 5.4(a) prohibits the attorney from sharing legal fees with a non-lawyer such as the physician. Although it may be factually accurate, A is an incorrect answer because the relationship of the attorney and the physician will violate MRPC 5.4(b). B is a wrong answer because a violation of MRPC 5.4(b) would occur even if the physician did not provide clients with legal advice.

QUESTION #97

A is the correct answer in this former clients conflict of interest situation that is governed by the Rules. The attorney should not represent the brother in his lawsuit against his sister because the attorney concurrently represented both of the partners in a substantially related case in which the brother's interests are materially adverse to the sister's interests. B is a wrong answer because the Rule still applies as stated in the foregoing sentence even if a different lawyer will represent the sister in the brother's lawsuit. C is an incorrect answer because the fact that the attorney did not receive the missing partnership information in the client's civil action does not fall under any exception to the conflict of interest Rules. D is a wrong answer because the reasonableness of the brother's belief that if the sister had provided the information, the results of litigation would have been different, is not dispositive

QUESTION #98

A is the correct answer because the commercial's contents would only be improper under MRPC 7.1 if the attorneys' conduct did not comply with the commercial. In other words, the commercial would violate the Rules by being false and misleading if the attorneys failed to abide by the terms of their offer by either charging people for the initial consultation or by failing to determine the fairness of the awards in domestic relations matters. B is a wrong answer because the commercial, by its terms, does not target people who are either represented or unrepresented by other counsel. C is an incorrect answer because MRPC 7.3(a) only prohibits the attorneys from directly contacting prospective clients by the following means: in-person, live telephone, or real-time electronic contact. Their radio commercial does not involve such direct solicitation of employment for economic gain. D is a wrong answer because the attorneys do not violate the Rules by requiring one to mention the commercial when arranging for an initial consultation in person while visiting their new office.

QUESTION #99

A is the correct answer because MRPC 3.5 prohibits the prosecutor, a lawyer, from communicating *ex parte* with a judge by her letter during this criminal proceeding. Although the trial had occurred, the proceeding was not finished because neither a judgment nor a potential sentencing had occurred. The facts do not indicate that either the law or a court order applied as an exception to authorize the prosecutor's letter. B is a wrong answer because the timing of the judge's issuance of the opinion is irrelevant to determining the letter's propriety. C is an incorrect answer because neither the facts nor MRPC 3.5 provides an exception on the basis that the prosecutor reasonably believed that a violation of the local speedy trial rule could have occurred. Although factually accurate, D is a wrong answer because the letter is improper regardless of whether the prosecutor sought to influence the judge.

QUESTION #100

D is the correct answer because the attorney violated MRPC 3.5, which prohibits him from seeking to influence the judge by legally prohibited means. A is a wrong answer because the attorney would be subject to discipline for violating that Rule even though he wrote the judge pursuant to the contractor's instructions. Although factually accurate, B is an incorrect answer because the facts do not indicate that state law either authorizes the attorney's letter to the judge or has any impact on the Rule's applicability. C is a wrong answer because the attorney's letter to the judge violated the Rule, regardless of the outcome of the prosecution of the contractor.

QUESTION #101

C is the correct answer because MRPC 1.15(e) requires the attorney to keep any disputed funds separate until the dispute is resolved.   Here, the attorney and the plaintiff dispute whether the plaintiff owes $3,000 in addition to the undisputed $7,000. But, the attorney failed to keep $3,000 separate by including it with the undisputed $7,000 when the attorney moved the $10,000 from the plaintiff's client trust account into his general account. In order to comply with the Rule, the attorney should have moved only $7,000 into the general account, and kept $3,000 in the client trust account until resolution of this dispute with the plaintiff occurred.

Note that the attorney would have violated another part of the Rule by not distributing to the plaintiff or himself any of the $75,000 until resolution of their dispute occurred. Specifically, in the event of a disputed claim, MRPC 1.15(e) requires that the attorney promptly distribute the remaining, undisputed portion of the property. Here, the attorney partially complied with that Rule by issuing the $65,000 check to the plaintiff and moving up to $7,000 into his general account. The attorney partially violated the Rule by moving the disputed $3,000 into his general account. In other words, the attorney could have fully complied with the Rule by moving only the undisputed $7,000 into his general account and leaving the disputed $3,000 in the plaintiff's client trust account until they resolved their dispute.

Although answers A and B are factually accurate, they are incorrect because they do not take into account the aforementioned effects of the Rule. Answer D is not correct because neither the parties' agreement nor the Rule provides that the attorney must receive the amount stated by the client.

QUESTION #102

C is the correct answer because MRPC 5.4(d) provides that the lawyer cannot practice with the other attorneys in their professional corporation because the family law attorney's wife, a non-lawyer, is its president. Therefore, A is a wrong answer because the Rule applies even if the lawyer was not an officer, shareholder, or member of the professional corporation and only held the status of a salaried employee. B is an incorrect answer because the Rule also applies even though the family law attorney's wife neither directs nor controls the professional judgment of any of the attorneys. D is a wrong answer because the Rule does not preclude the criminal defense attorney's husband from working as the firm's office assistant. Note that an exception to the Rule allows a fiduciary representative of a lawyer's estate to hold the lawyer's stock or interest for a reasonable time during administration.

QUESTION #103

A is the correct answer because it applies MRPC 8.2 (and 8.4(c)) to these facts. The attorney did not knowingly misrepresent any fact concerning the judge because he reasonably relied on the accuracy of the commission's letter. B is a wrong answer because it contradicts those provisions' prohibition against a candidate or opponent from knowingly making any misrepresentation about a candidate or opponent. C is an incorrect answer because its reason leads to the wrong conclusion and answer A provides the dispositive reason and correct conclusion. Although factually accurate, D is a wrong answer because the fact that the judge was actually disciplined for two instances of judicial conduct instead of one does not subject the attorney to discipline because he publicly stated the false information that the commission gave him.

QUESTION #104

B is the correct answer because it reflects MRPC 1.5. An attorney and client may enter into a reasonable contingency fee in most actions. A is a wrong answer because the plaintiff could properly request or suggest the terms and conditions of a contingency fee agreement. C is an incorrect answer, although at first glance, it is a tempting answer Under the comments to MRPC 1.8, a prohibited proprietary interest is treated differently from a contingency fee agreement. A contingency fee arrangement is permissible but the receipt of a property interest in the litigation is impermissible. In this case, therefore, the question turns on whether the attorney received a property interest in the litigation or entered into a contingency fee arrangement. The facts clearly state that the client suggested a "contingency fee arrangement" and agreed to pay 10% of the proceeds. It does not indicate that the attorney received a property interest. Therefore, because the plaintiff did not grant the attorney a proprietary interest in the civil action, the attorney's interest is a permissible contingency fee. This agreement is a classic example of a contingency fee arrangement permitted under MRPC 1.5. D is a wrong answer because the reasonableness of a contingency fee is not necessarily determined by comparing it to how much the attorney would have received by billing the plaintiff at a reasonable hourly rate.

QUESTION #105

A is the correct answer because MRPC 7.1 allows the attorney to publish the notice if it is true and does not contain any false or misleading statements. B is a wrong answer because, even if factually accurate, this answer is less than optimal. An attorney would be subject to discipline for publishing false information that is publicly available. C is an incorrect answer because the fact that the publication was made to people who had not been the attorney's clients does not violate the Rule. D is a wrong answer because the attorney's service as a legislator could have improved or increased his competence as an attorney. Nonetheless, it does not violate the rules to disclose service in the state legislature unless the disclosure implies the ability to unduly influence the legislative body.

QUESTION #106

D is the correct answer because the subordinate attorney cannot escape liability for violating an ethical rule simply as a result of following the directions of a supervisory attorney. C is a wrong answer because, although it accurately states that the supervising attorney's instructions to the subordinate attorney violated the ethical rules, the subordinate attorney is not liable simply because of the supervising attorney's violation of those rules. Rather, the subordinate attorney is liable because his conduct of destroying the documents violated those rules. A is an incorrect answer because the subordinate attorney's obedience to the supervising attorney's instructions does not enable the subordinate attorney to escape responsibility for violating the rules on the basis of a duty to obey the supervising attorney. This type of defense will not protect the subordinate attorney from his own conduct in violation of the ethical rules. Only if the subordinate attorney had destroyed the documents pursuant to the supervising attorney's reasonable resolution of a question of professional duty could A be a correct answer. However, the facts do not indicate that that occurred here. B is an incorrect answer because both the supervising attorney and the subordinate attorney violated an ethical rule.

QUESTION #107

Pursuant to MRPC 6.2(c), D is the correct answer because it describes a good cause for the attorney to avoid being appointed to represent the defendant based on her membership in the organization that assists domestic violence victims. C is a wrong answer because, although supported by MRPC 6.2(a), it is less dispositive than D and the attorney's representation of the defendant will not necessarily result in violating an ethical rule based on these facts. A is an incorrect answer because an attorney is not required to represent every person that the lawyer is appointed to represent. Although answer B describes a basis for the attorney not to represent the defendant, it is a wrong answer for two reasons. The first reason is that B states that representing the defendant *could impose* a financial burden upon the attorney, but MRPC 6.2(b) applies when representation *is likely to result* in an unreasonable financial burden on a lawyer. Second, the facts do not support this reason because, although the attorney incurs significant expense from her criminal defense work, she is not likely to suffer an unreasonable financial burden if either the court and/or the defendant must reimburse her for the costs of his legal defense. That can occur when a court appoints an attorney to represent a criminal defendant.

QUESTION #108

C is the correct answer because under these circumstances a court could find that a client-lawyer relationship existed for two reasons. First, the attorney took the prospective client's paperwork and told him not to be concerned about the arraignment. Second, the attorney made a delayed or "last minute" expression of an absence of intent to be retained by the prospective client. D is a wrong answer because an attorney s not always required to represent any client who requests representation. Rather, an attorney may decline to represent a client under certain circumstances. A is an incorrect answer because, as explained earlier, the facts give rise to a client-lawyer relationship between the prospective client and the attorney. B is a wrong answer because under certain situations, such as appointment of an attorney by a court, an attorney may not refuse to represent a client without showing good cause for that refusal.

QUESTION #109

The correct answer is D because the attorney complied with MRPC 1.5(b) by communicating the change to the manufacturer, which agreed to it. Thus, although answer B is factually accurate, it is a wrong answer because the manufacturer agreed to the change after initially opposing it. Even though answer A is factually accurate, the Rule recognizes that the attorney could change her billing rate during the representation, provided that she communicate that change to the manufacturer as happened here. Thus, C is incorrect because the fact that the attorney's business costs increased does not protect her from discipline for violating the Rule. Rather, that fact simply provides her reason for increasing her billing rate.

QUESTION #110

B is the correct answer because it accurately applies the dispositive ethical rule to the facts. The attorney, a lawyer whose personal friendship with the owner, a potential party litigant, could negatively impact his client relationship with the prospective client, can decline to represent the prospective client in litigation against the owner. This is a type of conflict of interest that could adversely affect the attorney's ability to provide proper representation. A is a wrong answer because it is too categorical when under certain circumstances, such as when a court appoints an attorney to represent a defendant, the attorney generally cannot avoid that representation without having good cause to do so. C is an incorrect answer because it is too categorical when, as here, an attorney is not required to represent every prospective client. D is a wrong answer because, even if it was factually accurate, B is more responsive to the question and directly applies the controlling ethical rule.

QUESTION #111

B is the correct answer because it accurately describes an exception to MRPC 1.8(c), which applies to these facts to allow the attorney to follow the client's instructions. A is a wrong answer because it is too categorical and contrary to the ethical rules, which only provide an exception for when, as here, the client is related to the lawyer. C is an incorrect answer because it is too categorical and does not provide for the exception for when, as here, the instrument makes a substantial gift to a lawyer related to the client. D is a wrong answer because the ethical rules permit the attorney to prepare this will, including its gift to her, because she is the client's relative.

QUESTION #112

C is the correct answer in this conflict of interest situation. The parties have followed the governing rule pursuant to which the attorney can render legal services to both the mortgagor and mortgagee. D is a wrong answer because the dispositive issue is whether the arrangement at issue complies with the rule, not whether it is common where the attorney works. Although it is factually accurate, A is an incorrect answer because the mortgagor's payment to the attorney does not render the attorney's preparation of the documents improper. B is a wrong answer because the fact that the interests of the mortgagor and mortgagee are different does not render their arrangement improper.

QUESTION #113

D is the correct answer because the attorney should have only moved $1,500 from the client trust account into the general account after she had earned $1,500 in legal fees. The controlling rule provides that an attorney could only move any of a client's retainer from the general account to the client trust account as fees are earned. Here, the attorney moved more of the retainer into the general account than she had earned and had to return $750 that she had not earned. The attorney should have only moved $1,500, rather than $3,000 initially, and only $750 after performing the other five hours of work.

A is a wrong answer because the attorney should have initially only moved $1,500 and she should have only moved $750 after having earned it by working another 5 hours. By taking that approach, the attorney would not have needed to return $750 to the client trust account. B is an incorrect answer because under the rule it does not matter if the attorney legitimately expected to perform another 10 more hours of work on the client's matter the next day. An attorney can only move funds from the client trust account to the general account after they are earned. C is a wrong answer because the attorney properly withdrew $1,500 from the general account that she had placed there after completing the first 10 hours of legal work for the client.

QUESTION #114

B is the correct answer because it would be permissible for the attorney to contact the client when the attorney previously represented the client and the contact concerned the subject matter of the representation. A is an incorrect answer because the attorney is not precluded from subsequently preparing a new lease for the client after having prepared the original lease. C is a wrong answer because, even if a basis existed for the attorney to think that the client obtained other counsel, the attorney would be contacting the client regarding the subject matter of the previous representation. D is an incorrect answer because the attorney would be contacting the client to provide information regarding the change in the law, not necessarily to solicit legal business.

QUESTION #115

B is the correct answer because an attorney representing a client before a legislative body or administrative agency in a non-adjudicative proceeding must disclose that the appearance is in a representative capacity. A is a wrong answer because an attorney can receive compensation for attempting to affect legislative action. C is an incorrect answer because whether the attorney sincerely thought that he advanced a position that served the public interest is not dispositive here or relevant under the rule. D is a wrong answer because, even if the legislature was only concerned with the nature of the testimony instead of the source of a witness's compensation, the rule requires that the attorney disclose that the appearance is in a representative capacity.

QUESTION #116

C is the correct answer because it reflects the governing rule allowing for dual representation that would not result in a significant risk that the interests of either partner would be materially prejudiced. D is a wrong answer because the fact that attorney had already been representing both partners with respect to their partnership is not a valid basis under the rule for their dual representation in terms of criminal liability. A is an incorrect answer because the permissibility of the attorney's dual representation is not conditional upon the waiver of client-lawyer confidentiality by both partners. B is a wrong answer because the rule does not require the attorney to notify the partners that they should contact independent counsel before they signed and returned his letter to them.

QUESTION #117

A is the correct answer because the controlling rule prohibits the contracts attorney from representing the seller's legal representative when it is likely that the contracts attorney will be a necessary witness whose testimony would relate to the contested issue of the purchaser's mental competency. D is a wrong answer because it states the opposite of an exception that would only allow the contracts attorney to testify if his testimony related to an uncontested issue. B is an incorrect answer because the rule does not provide that the mere fact that the contracts attorney drafted the contract precludes the contracts attorney from representing the seller. The rule applies if the contracts attorney is likely to be a necessary witness, but the rule is subject to exceptions, the application of which depends upon the factual situation in question. C is a wrong answer because the fact that the contracts attorney is the only witness still alive is not an exception to the rule.

QUESTION #118

A is the correct answer because the attorney cannot represent the accountant in an action in which the attorney will testify, and the testimony will relate to a contested issue in the case. MRPC 3.7(a) provides that an attorney may serve as an advocate and a necessary witness who testifies in the same trial if "(1) the testimony relates to an uncontested issue; (2) the testimony relates to the nature and value of legal services rendered in the case; or (3) disqualification of the" attorney would result in substantial hardship to the client. In this case, the mental competence of the client will be the pivotal contested issue in the will contest. Although it is factually accurate, C is an incorrect answer because the attorney's status as the only available subscribing witness is of no legal consequence to the attorney's ability to be a witness. D is incorrect because there is no rule providing that the attorney could be a witness, or avoid being a witness, even if the receptionist was found and made available to testify. B is incorrect because there is no such law.

QUESTION #119

Answer choice C is correct. This question tests Model Rule 6.2, which addresses the circumstances in which an attorney may seek to avoid a representation directed by a court or other tribunal. Under Rule 6.2, a lawyer *must not* seek to avoid appointment by a tribunal to represent a person except for good cause. Good cause exists if: (1) representing the client is likely to result in violation of the Rules or other law; (2) representing the client is likely to result in an unreasonable financial burden on the lawyer; or (3) the client or the cause is so repugnant to the lawyer as to be likely to impair the client-lawyer relationship or the lawyer's ability to represent the client. Thus, unless there is a real likelihood that the appointment will present an unreasonable financial burden on the attorney – for example, because the case will require all of her attention for a substantial period of time, thus preventing her from working on any income-producing cases – the mere possibility that potential clients may not seek out the attorney's services is insufficient to justify seeking to decline the appointment.

Answer choice A is incorrect because it is not enough that the attorney strongly dislikes the crime with which the defendant has been charged. Under Model Rule 6.2(c), the attorney cannot seek to avoid the appointment unless her distaste for the client or his cause is so strong as to impair the client-lawyer relationship or the attorney's ability to represent the client. Here, the facts indicate that although the attorney has strong feelings about the client's case, she is confident that she can ably represent him.

Answer choice B is incorrect because the fact that she has not established an attorney-client relationship with the defendant is irrelevant. The attorney is obliged to accept the representation unless good cause exists to avoid the appointment. Model Rule 6.2; Restatement of the Law Governing Lawyers, Third, § 14(2).

Answer choice D is incorrect because the Model Rules do not require the attorney to obtain the defendant's informed, written consent to decline the appointment.

QUESTION #120

Answer choice A is correct. Under Model Rule 1.5(a), a lawyer may not charge an unreasonable fee. In evaluating whether a fee is unreasonable, several factors are to be considered, including: (1) the time and labor required, the difficulty of the issues involved, and the skill required to perform the legal service; (2) the likelihood that taking on the case will preclude other employment by the lawyer; (3) the fee customarily charged in the locality for similar legal services; (4) the amount involved and the results obtained; (5) the time limitations imposed by the circumstances or the client; (6) the nature and length of the professional relationship with the client; (7) the experience, reputation, and ability of the lawyer; and (8) whether the fee is contingent. *Id.* A lawyer's fee agreement should be communicated to the client, preferably in writing. Rule 1.5(b). Although contingent fees are acceptable in some cases, *see* Rule 1.5(c), in no circumstance may a lawyer charge a fee in any domestic relations matter where the fee is contingent on the securing of a divorce or the amount of alimony or support awarded or settlement agreement reached. Rule 1.5(d)(1). Here, the lawyer's fee appears reasonable, given his reputation and the fact that the fee is not substantially higher than fees charged by less experienced lawyers in the area. Although the lawyer has agreed to defer receipt of his fee until after the case is over, neither the amount of his fee nor its receipt is contingent on securing a divorce or obtaining any amount of money or property for the wife.

Answer choice B is incorrect because the lawyer's fee is not contingent upon the securing of a divorce or upon the amount of alimony or support, or property settlement. Model Rule 1.5(d)(1).

Answer choice C is incorrect because, as explained above, the lawyer is not charging a contingency fee. Even if he were charging a contingency fee, the fact that the agreement has been reduced to writing and that the wife has signed it is irrelevant. Model Rule 1.5(d) strictly prohibits contingency fees in divorce proceedings.

Answer choice D is incorrect because the facts do not suggest that his fee is *per se* unreasonable. Model Rule 1.5(a) presents several factors to consider when determining whether a fee is unreasonably high. As explained above, the lawyer in this case is experienced and has a good reputation, and his hourly fee does not appear substantially higher than the fees charged by less experienced lawyers in the area for similar legal work.

QUESTION #121

Answer choice B is correct. This question tests Model Rule 1.9(a), which governs when an attorney may represent a client whose interests are materially adverse to those of a former client in the same or a substantially related matter. Under Rule 1.9(a), such a representation is impermissible unless the former client gives informed, written consent. Answer choice B reflects the fact that the owner has provided oral consent to the representation, not written consent.

Answer choice A is incorrect because the representation would not involve a concurrent conflict of interest, since the lawyer's representation of the owner concluded when the labor dispute was resolved.

Answer choice C is incorrect because the owner's oral consent to the representation is insufficient. Rule 1.9(a) requires the former client to give informed, *written* consent.

Answer choice D is incorrect because the lawyer's acquisition of information during the previous lawsuit that could hurt the owner in the busboys' suit does not preclude him from taking on the busboys as clients. However, the lawyer is still subject to the provisions of Model Rule 1.9(c), which govern his ability to use the damaging information against the owner.

QUESTION #122

Answer choice C is correct. This question tests Model Rule 5.1, which explains when a lawyer will be subject to discipline for a subordinate lawyer's misconduct, and Model Rule 1.15 which sets forth an attorney's duty to safeguard a client's property. Under Rule 1.15(a), a lawyer must keep a client's property separate from the lawyer's own property, such as in a client trust account. Money earned by a lawyer must then be paid from the client trust account. Under Model Rule 5.1(c), a supervising attorney is subject to discipline for a subordinate attorney's misconduct if the supervising lawyer: (1) orders or, with knowledge of the specific conduct, ratifies the conduct involved; or (2) knows of the conduct at a time when its consequences can be avoided or mitigated but fails to take reasonable remedial action. Here, the associate has violated Rule 1.15 because he did not deposit all of the client's funds in the trust account before deducting the fees owed to the firm. However, the managing partner is not subject to discipline for the associate's conduct because, as the facts indicate, he properly trained the associate to handle client funds and did not know that the associate failed to deposit the settlement check in the client trust account.

Answer choice A is incorrect because, as explained above, the associate is subject to discipline for violating Rule 1.15.

Answer choice B is incorrect on both points, as explained above.

Answer choice D is incorrect because the managing partner did not violate Rule 5.1(c).

QUESTION #123

Answer choice D is correct. This question tests Model Rules 5.4 and 7.2. Under Rule 7.2(b)(4), a lawyer may enter into a reciprocal referral agreement provided that: (i) the agreement is not exclusive; and (ii) the referred client is informed of the existence and nature of the agreement. Here, the attorney and entrepreneur have entered into an exclusive reciprocal referral agreement, thus violating Rule 7.2.

Answer choice A is incorrect. Under Model Rule 5.4(b), a lawyer may not form a partnership with a non-lawyer if any of the activities of the partnership consist of the practice of law. This choice correctly notes that none of the resource center's services amounts to the practice of law, but it overlooks the fact that, as explained above, the attorney has violated Model Rule 7.2.

Answer choice B is incorrect. Rule 5.4(b) limits a lawyer's ability to form a partnership with non-lawyers so as to preserve a lawyer's professional independence.

Answer choice C is incorrect because it overstates the applicable rule: Model Rule 5.4(b) allows an attorney to enter into a partnership with a non-lawyer, provided that the partnership does not practice law in any way.

QUESTION #124

Answer choice B is correct. Under Model Rule 7.3(a), a lawyer may not "solicit professional employment from a prospective client when a significant motive for the lawyer's doing so is the lawyer's pecuniary gain . . . ." An exception to Rule 7.3(a) exists if the prospective client is a lawyer, *see* Model Rule 7.3(a)(1), provided that the prospective client has not made known to the lawyer a desire not to be solicited and that the solicitation does not involve coercion, duress, or harassment. Model Rule 7.3(b). Here, the lawyer solicited business from a lawyer, and nothing in the facts suggests that he coerced her or harassed her, or that she was under duress.

Answer choice A is incorrect because it overstates the applicable rule. Model Rule 7.3(a) allows a lawyer to solicit business for pecuniary gain from a lawyer or someone with whom the soliciting attorney has a family, close personal, or prior professional relationship, provided that the restrictions of Rule 7.3(b) are not violated.

Answer choice C is incorrect. Although the lawyer should not *take on the representation* because he is a potential witness, *see* Model Rule 3.7(a), Rule 7.3 does not prohibit his solicitation on that basis. Nor does the attorney's reasonable belief about the merits of the case impact the propriety of his solicitation.

Answer choice D is incorrect. Model Rule 7.3(b) prohibits an attorney from soliciting business from a prospective client – even if the solicitation is not barred by Rule 7.3(a) – if the prospective client has made known to the lawyer that he or she does not want to receive solicitations. Although the facts here indicate that the driver of the station wagon disapproved of the solicitation in hindsight, nothing in the fact pattern suggests that she gave the personal injury attorney any indication that she did not want to be solicited.

QUESTION #125

Answer choice D is correct. This question tests Model Rules 1.11 and 7.5. Under Model Rule 1.11, a lawyer serving as a public official may practice law, provided that he does not violate Rule 1.7 or Rule 1.9, which govern conflicts of interest. Under Rule 7.5(c), if an attorney practicing in a firm takes public office, the firm may continue to use the public official's name in the firm name, provided that the attorney/public official continues to actively and regularly practice with the firm. Here, the lawyer has avoided any conflict of interest between his role as a legislator and his role as an attorney, and thus has not violated any of the Model Rules in that regard. Because the facts indicate that he continues to practice with the firm actively and regularly (albeit with some additional help from his partners), the firm has not violated Rule 7.5(c) by continuing to use his name.

Answer choice A is incorrect on both accounts. As explained above, the partner/legislator may practice law as long as he complies with the rules governing conflicts of interest. And the firm may continue to use the partner's name during his term in the legislature as long as he actively and regularly practices with the firm.

Answer choice B is incorrect because, as discussed above, the partner's name does not need to be removed from the firm's name.

Answer choice C is incorrect because the partner/legislator may continue to practice in the firm, subject to Rules 1.7, 1.9, and 1.11. Moreover, if the partner ceased working at the firm because of his role in the legislature, the firm would violate Rule 7.5(c) by retaining his name in the firm's name.

QUESTION #126

Answer choice C is correct. This question tests Model Rule 7.2. Under that Rule, a lawyer generally "shall not give anything of value to a person for recommending the lawyer's services . . . ." Rule 7.2(b). Exceptions to this Rule exist if the lawyer: (1) pays the reasonable costs of otherwise permissible advertisements or communications; (2) pays the charges of a legal service plan, non-profit, or qualified lawyer referral service; (3) is purchasing a law practice; or (4) is making a referral pursuant to a permissible reciprocal referral agreement. *Id.*

Answer choice A is incorrect. Model Rule 5.4 does prohibit a lawyer from sharing legal fees with a non-lawyer. However, that is not the case here. The lawyer has given his neighbor – a non-lawyer – the gift of a bottle of wine, which is distinct from a portion of the client's fees.

Answer choice B is incorrect because, under Model Rule 7.2(b), a lawyer may not give *anything* of value to a person in exchange for a referral unless the lawyer does so in compliance with one of four exceptions in Rule 7.2(b). Here, none of those exceptions has been satisfied, and the per se rule applies regardless of how reasonable the gift may seem.

Answer choice D is incorrect for the same reason as answer choice B: the value of the item given in exchange for a referral is irrelevant. The lawyer violates Rule 7.2(b) unless his conduct falls into one of the Rule's four exceptions.

QUESTION #127

Answer choice A is correct. Under Code of Judicial Conduct ("CJC") Rule 3.11(A), a judge may hold investments. Under Rule 3.11(B), a judge may participate in a business closely held by the judge or members of his family. A judge's ability to participate in these financial activities is limited, however, by Rule 3.11(C), which prevents a judge from doing so if his involvement will: (1) interfere with his judicial duties; (2) lead to frequent disqualification of the judge; (3) involve the judge in frequent transactions or continuing business relationships with lawyers or other persons likely to come before the court on which the judge serves; or (4) result in other violations of the Code of Judicial Conduct. Here, the facts do not indicate that any of the restrictions in Rule 3.11(C) have been violated. Thus, the judge may continue to hold company stock and serve on the board of directors.

Answer choice B is incorrect because, although the company is mired in state court litigation, such litigation does not occur in the judge's state, let alone before his court. Thus, there is no chance that he will be disqualified, and it is unlikely that other persons involved with the business will appear frequently before the judge's court.

Answer choice C is incorrect. Although CJC Rule 3.11(C)(1) requires a judge to cease financial activities that interfere with the performance of his or her judicial duties, the facts here indicate that the judge's involvement with the company will not interfere with his judicial duties. His involvement requires only a few days per year, and no conflicts of interest appear likely to arise.

Answer choice D is incorrect because CJC Rule 3.11 allows a judge to participate in running a business with his family members, provided certain conditions are met. Nothing in Rule 3.11 requires that the other participants in the business be lawyers.

QUESTION #128

Answer choice C is correct. This question tests Model Rule 4.2, which prohibits a lawyer from communicating about the subject of the representation with another party in a matter if: (1) the other party is represented by counsel, and (2) the lawyer has not first obtained consent to the communication from the other party's lawyer. The lawyer need not get consent from the other party's lawyer if the communication is authorized under the law or by court order. Here, the lawyer has not obtained the consent of the wife's lawyer, and the facts do not indicate that the law or a court order allow him to contact the wife regarding the divorce proceedings.

Answer choice A is incorrect because the client's interest and approval are irrelevant to the attorney's duty to abide by Rule 4.2.

Answer choice B is incorrect for similar reasons: the wife's consent, like the lawyer's intent, is irrelevant under Rule 4.2, which is designed to prevent attorneys from interfering with the interests of a represented party.

Answer choice D is incorrect because it overstates the limitations in Rule 4.2. Although a lawyer generally may not contact a represented party in a matter about the subject of the representation without first getting consent from that party's lawyer, the Comments to Rule 4.2 indicate that this prohibition does not apply to communications concerning a matter outside of the representation.

QUESTION #129

Answer choice A is correct. This question tests Model Rule of Professional Conduct 3.4, which requires a lawyer to demonstrate fairness towards an opposing party and opposing counsel. Under Rule 3.4(f), a lawyer may not request of a person who is not his client that the person refrain from voluntarily giving relevant information to another party unless: (1) the person is a relative, employee, or other agent of the client; and (2) the lawyer reasonably believes that the person's interests will not be adversely affected by refraining from giving such information. Here, the lawyer has requested that the son not volunteer information that relates to his mother's lawsuit, and there is nothing in the fact pattern that suggests the son's interests would be adversely affected by withholding such information, provided he does not do so in violation of the law.

Answer choice B is incorrect because Rule 3.4(f) allows a lawyer to make such a request of a non-client in certain circumstances.

Answer choice C is incorrect because it overlooks the permissive nature of Rule 3.4(f). Although certain circumstances may arise in which the opposing party can demand access to relevant information, such as during discovery and at trial, the attorney may request that his client's son not volunteer relevant information unless and until such an obligation arises.

Answer choice D is a red herring. The son is not the lawyer's client, so he is not entitled to the protections of Model Rule 1.6. Since the interview in which the son told the lawyer about his mother was not a consultation about the possibility of forming a client-lawyer relationship, the son's communications to the lawyer are not privileged under Model Rule 1.18. Since no attorney-client relationship was formed with the son, the lawyer could be subject to discipline for his request unless the request fell under the exception set forth in Rule 3.4(f).

QUESTION #130

Answer choice D is correct. This question tests Model Rule 1.6. Under Rule 1.6(a), a lawyer generally must keep confidential information given by a client relating to the representation. There are several exceptions to this Rule that allow a lawyer to disclose confidential information at the lawyer's discretion. Under Rule 1.6(b)(1), a lawyer may – but does not have to -- reveal confidential information to the extent that the lawyer reasonably believes necessary "to prevent reasonably certain death or substantial bodily harm[.]" The facts in this question indicate that the client has a history of aggression towards his former partner and is especially angry. Although the owner has made a statement to his attorney in confidence, the facts suggest that he is likely to harm his former partner with a gun. Under the circumstances, Rule 1.6(b) would permit the attorney to disclose his client's statement and actions to prevent the death of or substantial injury to the former partner.

Answer choices A and B are incorrect because the circumstances indicate that an exception to Rule 1.6(a) exists, but the exception makes the attorney's disclosure permissible, not mandatory.

Answer choice C is incorrect because the Model Rules do not require that an attorney consult with bar counsel before making a disclosure permitted by Rule 1.6(b). Of course, the attorney *may* first seek advice from bar counsel concerning his obligations under the Rules of Professional Conduct. *See* Model Rule 1.6(b)(4).

QUESTION #131

Answer choice B is correct. This question tests Model Rule of Professional Conduct ("MRPC") 3.5 and Model Code of Judicial Conduct ("CJC") Rule 2.9. Under MRPC 3.5, a lawyer is prohibited from making an ex parte communication, which is a communication made to a judge for or by one party outside the presence of the other party, unless the communication is authorized by law or court order. MRPC 3.5(b). Judges are similarly barred from initiating, permitting, or considering ex parte communications concerning a pending matter under CJC Rule 2.9. However, CJC Rule 2.9(A)(1) allows a judge to participate in an ex parte communication for scheduling, administrative, or emergency purposes, provided that: "(a) the judge reasonably believes that no party will gain a procedural, substantive, or tactical advantage as a result of the ex parte communication; and (b) the judge makes provision promptly to notify all other parties of the substance of the ex parte communication, and gives the parties an opportunity to respond." Here, the defense attorney's request to adjust the day's schedule, though made ex parte, did not violate MRPC Rule 3.5 because the facts indicate that such a request is permissible under the state's laws. Likewise, the judge's ex parte discussion with the defense attorney does not appear to violate CJC Rule 2.9. It concerned a scheduling matter that did not appear to give one party an advantage over the other, and the judge immediately notified the plaintiff's attorney of the request and allowed him to respond.

Answer choice A is incorrect. The MRPC prohibits ex parte communications by lawyers, regardless of who initiates them. Likewise, the CJC prohibits judges from any involvement in an impermissible ex parte communication. *See* CJC Rule 2.9(A) ("A judge shall not initiate, permit, or consider ex parte communications . . . ."). However, as explained above, the lawyer's ex parte communication with the judge was permissible under state law, and the judge did not violate the CJC.

Answer choice C is incorrect. The conversation between the defendant's attorney and the judge was clearly ex parte. However, the ex parte conversation did not violate the MRPC or CJC.

Answer choice D is incorrect because, as explained above, some ex parte communications are permitted under the MRCP and CJC. *See* MRPC 3.5; CJC Rule 2.9(A)(1)-(5).

QUESTION #132

Answer choice A is correct. This question tests Model Rule 4.3, which regulates an attorney's communications with unrepresented persons. Under Rule 4.3, an attorney for one party may not give legal advice, other than the advice to secure counsel, to an unrepresented person if the lawyer knows or reasonably should know that the unrepresented person's interests are in conflict with, or have a reasonable possibility of being in conflict with, the interests of the attorney's client. Here, the attorney advised the neighbor, who he knew to be unrepresented, and whose interests were clearly adverse to those of the attorney's client, that (1) he should consider obtaining a lawyer and (2) that his proposed countersuit was meritless. Although the attorney acted properly in advising the neighbor to consider getting a lawyer, it was impermissible for the attorney to advise him on the proposed countersuit.

Answer choice B is incorrect because an attorney is not per se barred from contacting an unrepresented person. As explained above, however, certain communications by an attorney to an unrepresented person are impermissible under Rule 4.3.

Answer choice C is incorrect because the attorney's belief about the merits of his legal advice, reasonable or not, is irrelevant. Rule 4.3 prohibits an attorney, in dealing with an unrepresented person, from implying that he is disinterested in a matter. This Rule becomes particularly important when the interests of the attorney's client are adverse to those of the unrepresented person. As Comment [2] to Rule 4.3 notes, the danger that a lawyer will compromise the interests of an unrepresented party whose interests are adverse to those of the lawyer's client is so high that the lawyer may not provide any advice on the matter whatsoever, save for the advice that the unrepresented party should obtain counsel.

Answer choice D is incorrect for similar reasons. Even if the neighbor genuinely intended to proceed without a lawyer, the homeowner's attorney violated Rule 4.3 by giving the neighbor any legal advice beyond the advice that he obtain counsel.

QUESTION #133

Answer choice B is correct. This question tests Model Rule 1.9, which governs an attorney's duties to former clients. Under Rule 1.9(a), an attorney who formerly represented one party may not then represent a second party "in the same or a substantially related matter in which that person's interests are materially adverse to the interests of the former client unless the former client gives informed consent, confirmed in writing." The key issue in this question is whether the tenants' case is the same or a substantially related matter. As Comment [3] to Rule 1.9 explains, matters are "'substantially related' . . . if they involve the same transaction or legal dispute or if there otherwise is a substantial risk that confidential factual information as would normally have been obtained in the prior representation would materially advance the client's position in the matter." Given the facts in this question, it does not appear that the tenants' case and the lawyer's original representation are substantially related. They are separate legal actions, the lawyer's involvement in the re-zoning matter ended before the condos were constructed, and there is no indication that he had any knowledge about the way the condos would be built. Thus, there is no conflict of interest and the lawyer may take the tenants' case.

Answer choice A is incorrect because the tenants' interests are plainly adverse to those of the lawyer's former client. Thus, the lawyer may not represent the tenants unless their case is not a "substantially related matter" or, if it is, he obtains the developer's informed, written consent.

Answer choice C is incorrect because the lawyer would only need the developer's informed, written consent if the lawyer was representing the tenants against the developer in a matter substantially related to the original representation.

Answer choice D is incorrect because, although the tenants' interests are materially adverse to those of the lawyer's former client, that is not enough to preclude the lawyer from representing the tenants. Under Rule 1.9, he may do so if the tenants' case is not the same or a substantially related matter. Moreover, he could still represent the tenants against the developer in the same or a substantially related matter if the developer provided informed, written consent.

QUESTION #134

Answer choice D is correct. This question tests Model Rule of Professional Conduct 3.6. Under Rule 3.6(a), an attorney participating in the investigation or litigation of a matter may not make an out-of-court statement that he knows or reasonably should know is likely to be disseminated publicly and is substantially likely to materially prejudice an adjudicative proceeding in the matter. The Rule contains several exceptions, such as: statements that an investigation of a matter is in progress; requests for assistance in obtaining evidence and information necessary to the matter; and warnings of danger concerning the person involved, if there is reason to believe that there exists a likelihood of substantial harm to an individual or the public interest. *See* Rule 3.6(b)(3, 5-6). In addition, an attorney participating in a criminal case may also make public statements requesting information necessary to aid in the apprehension of an accused individual. *See* Rule 3.6(b)(7)(ii). Here, most of the prosecutor's statements are permitted under Rule 3.6(b). However, the prosecutor also commented that the defendant's flight was clear evidence of his guilt, a statement which is likely to prejudice the potential jury pool against the defendant. Indeed, Comment [5(4)] to Rule 3.6 specifically identifies "any opinion as to the guilt or innocence of a defendant . . . in a criminal case" as a statement that is more likely than not to have a material prejudicial effect on the proceeding.

Answer choice A is incorrect. Although Model Rule 3.6(b)(6) indicates that a lawyer participating in a matter may make a public statement about a defendant's behavior that relates to public safety if a substantial likelihood of danger exists, a lawyer must balance such statements to avoid prejudice. In this case, the prosecutor may not be subject to discipline for alerting the public to a danger posed by the defendant, if there existed a reason to believe that the defendant likely posed such a danger. Even so, the prosecutor should not have used his warning as an opportunity to comment on his belief in the defendant's guilt. *See* Comment [5(4)] to Rule 3.6.

Answer choice B is incorrect because the prosecutor's *adversarial* role is irrelevant. Under Rule 3.6, no attorney participating in a proceeding, including the prosecutor, may make any public statement that would materially prejudice the defendant. As explained above, the prosecutor's public statement concerning the defendant's guilt was prohibited by Rule 3.6.

Answer choice C is incorrect because it overstates Rule 3.6. Although an attorney participating a matter may not make statements that would materially prejudice the matter, Rule 3.6(b) provides a list of statements that an attorney may make regarding a proceeding, including statements related to criminal proceedings. Moreover, this list is not exhaustive. *See* Comment [4] to Rule 3.6.

QUESTION #135

Answer choice C is correct. This question tests Model Rule 5.6, under which a lawyer may not offer or make an employment agreement limiting the right of a lawyer to practice law after termination of the relationship. An exception to this Rule exists with respect to agreements concerning benefits upon retirement. Here, the proposed contract provision runs afoul of Rule 5.6 because, in preventing the corporate attorney from working for the lawyer's former partner in any capacity, the restriction necessarily limits the corporate attorney's ability to practice law upon termination of the employment relationship with the lawyer.

Answer choice A is incorrect because it overlooks the prohibition in Rule 5.6, which exists to protect a lawyer's professional independence.

Answer choice B is incorrect because a conflict of interest is not created simply because a lawyer leaves one firm for a competitor's law firm. And there is nothing in the facts suggesting that an actual or potential conflict of interest would arise if the corporate attorney joined the former partner's firm.

Answer choice D is incorrect because a restriction on an attorney's future ability to practice law is impermissible whether the restriction is proposed by the employer or the employee. Model Rule 5.6 ("A lawyer shall not participate in *offering or making*" an agreement limiting the lawyer's future ability to practice law.) (emphasis added).

QUESTION #136

Answer choice A is correct. This question tests CJC Rule 2.13 and, to a lesser extent, Rule 1.2. Rule 1.2 requires a judge to "act at all times in a manner that promotes public confidence in the independence, integrity, and impartiality of the judiciary, and shall avoid impropriety and the appearance of impropriety." This requirement extends to the manner in which a judge makes administrative appointments, including the selection of a judge's personnel, such as clerks, secretaries, and bailiffs. *See* CJC Rule 2.13(A), and Comment [1] thereto. Accordingly, Rule 2.13(A) requires a judge to avoid nepotism, favoritism, and unnecessary appointments. Comment [2] to Rule 2.3 defines nepotism as "the appointment or hiring of any relative within the third degree of either the judge or the judge's spouse or domestic partner, or the spouse or domestic partner of such relative." As explained in the Terminology section of the CJC, the "third degree of relationship" includes: "great-grandparent, grandparent, uncle, aunt, brother, sister, child, grandchild, great-grandchild, nephew, and niece." Here, the judge would violate CJC Rule 2.13(A) if he hires his niece as a clerk.

Answer choice B is incorrect because, although a judge may exercise considerable control when making administrative appointments, the judge must do so impartially and on the basis of merit, CJC Rule 2.13(A)(1), and avoid nepotism, favoritism and unnecessary appointments. Rule 2.13(A)(2).

Answer choice C is incorrect. A judge must exercise the power of appointment based on merit, *see* Rule 2.13(A)(1), and the facts indicate that the judge's niece is highly qualified for the clerkship position. However, a judge must also avoid nepotism. *See* Rule 2.13(A)(2). Thus, notwithstanding his niece's qualifications, the judge would violate the Code of Judicial Conduct if he hires her.

Answer choice D is incorrect for two reasons. First, the Code of Judicial Conduct has no requirement that a judge hire the "most qualified" applicant for a position. Indeed, it would be difficult to define what characteristics make any applicant the "most qualified." Rule 2.13(A) simply requires that personnel be hired based on merit. More fundamentally, whether a job applicant is the most qualified person or not, a judge may not hire an applicant if he or she is within the third degree of relationship, as the niece is in this fact pattern.

QUESTION #137

Answer choice C is correct. This question tests Model Rule 7.4, which governs a lawyer's communications regarding his fields of practice and specialization. A lawyer may communicate that he does or does not practice a particular field of law, *see* Rule 7.4(a), and may generally state that he is a "specialist," "specializes in," or "practices a specialty" in a particular field or fields, provided that such statement is not false or misleading. *See* Comment [1] to Rule 7.4. Here, the lawyer has decided to limit his practice to immigration and citizenship matters, and he appears to have a sufficient background studying immigration and citizenship law such that his decision to advertise as "specializing" in that field is not false or materially misleading, even if he has previously handled only one immigration case.

Answer choice A is incorrect. Rule 7.4 and the Comments thereto distinguish between an indication that an attorney specializes in a particular field of law, on one hand, and an indication that an attorney has been *certified* by an organization as a specialist in a field of law, on the other. Under Rule 7.4(d), the former is impermissible unless the certifying organization has been approved by proper authorities and is identified in the lawyer's communication. Comment [3] to Rule 7.4 highlights the difference: unlike the general statement that a lawyer specializes in a particular field, "[c]ertification signifies that an objective entity has recognized an advanced degree of knowledge and experience in the specialty area greater than is suggested by general licensure to practice law."

Answer choice B is incorrect because it misstates Rule 7.4. As explained above, Rule 7.4 generally permits lawyers to communicate the fact that they do or do not practice in particular fields of law, and they may do so by stating that they "specialize" in a particular field, provided that the statement is not false or misleading. Rule 7.4 contains special provisions for patent lawyers and admiralty lawyers, allowing such lawyers to use special designations other than "specialist." *See* Rule 7.4(b), (c).

Answer choice D is incorrect. The fact that this attorney has only handled one immigration case before is arguably relevant to the question whether his use of the term "specializes" is false or misleading. However, the facts indicate that he has studied immigration and citizenship law extensively and that he is reasonably confident in his ability to practice that field of law. Thus, the facts above do not give rise to the conclusion that the lawyer's advertisement is false or misleading.

QUESTION #138

Answer choice B is correct. This question tests CJC Rule 3.6, which prohibits judges from affiliating with discriminatory organizations. Under Rule 3.6(B), a judge may "not use the benefits or facilities of an organization if the judge knows or should know that the organization practices invidious discrimination on one or more grounds," including race. However, a judge's attendance at an event in a facility of such an organization does not violate Rule 3.6 if the attendance: (1) is an isolated event that (2) could not reasonably be perceived as an endorsement of the organization's discriminatory practices. The facts in this question indicate that this is an isolated event – a single dinner – at a club that the fraternity has not been involved with before, and which discriminates based on an "unwritten policy" of which neither the fraternity member who made the reservation nor the judge are aware. Moreover, the guests in attendance at the dinner, including some of the honorees, are African-American, suggesting that the fraternity is inclusive and that neither its current members nor its alumni endorse the club's practices. Thus, the judge's attendance would not appear to violate Rule 3.6.

Answer choice A is incorrect because, even if the club is private and cannot constitutionally be prohibited from discriminating in its membership, the judge could violate the CJC if his attendance in the club's facilities could be viewed as an endorsement of the club's invidious discrimination against African-Americans. *See* CJC Rule 3.6(B).

Answer choice C is incorrect. That the club discriminates on the basis of race is not enough, on its own, to render the judge's attendance at an event in the club a violation of the CJC. Rather, his attendance must reasonably suggest that he endorses the club's discriminatory practices. *See* Rule 3.6(B).

Answer choice D is incorrect because the judge is not prohibited from accepting the dinner. CJC Rule 3.13 prohibits a judge from accepting any gift that is unlawful or "would appear to a reasonable person to undermine the judge's independence, integrity, or impartiality." Rule 3.13(A). However, a judge may accept an invitation to an event related to an extrajudicial activity the judge is involved in – such as a fraternal organization – "if the same invitation is offered to non-judges who are engaged in similar ways in the activity as is the judge," provided that the judge complies with the gift reporting requirements in CJC Rule 3.15. Rule 3.13(C)(2)(b). The dinner in this fact pattern falls within the ambit of Rule 3.13(C), and the judge therefore would not violate the Code of Judicial Conduct by attending the dinner.

QUESTION #139

Answer choice D is correct. This question tests Model Rules 1.17 and 5.4. Under Rule 1.17, which governs the sale of a law practice, a lawyer may purchase a practice (and, in turn, a lawyer may sell a practice) if: the seller ceases to engage in the practice of law; the practice is sold, in whole or in part, to a lawyer, lawyers, or law firms; the seller notifies all of the practice's existing clients of the sale, that they may take possession of their files or retain other counsel, and that their consent to transfer the files will be presumed if no answer is received within 90 days; and the fees charged to clients are not increased by reason of the sale. As Comment [13] to Rule 1.17 explains, the Rule contemplates the sale of a practice by a non-lawyer representing a deceased attorney's estate, and such a practice is permissible because the purchasing lawyer will ensure compliance with the applicable Rules. And as Model Rule 5.4 explains, a lawyer who purchases the law practice of a deceased lawyer may pay the agreed-upon purchase price to the deceased lawyer's estate, provided that the purchasing lawyer otherwise complies with Rule 1.17.

Answer choice A is incorrect because, as Comment [13] to Rule 1.17 explains, a lawyer may purchase a law practice from a non-lawyer who represents the estate of a deceased lawyer.

Answer choice B is incorrect because the ultimate beneficiary of the sale of a law practice is irrelevant. A lawyer may purchase a law practice from a deceased lawyer's estate, and nothing in the Model Rules prohibits the proceeds of such a sale from being distributed by the estate in accordance with the deceased lawyer's wishes.

Answer choice C is incorrect because the practice's clients need not agree to keep their business with the purchasing attorney in order to validate the sale of the practice. Indeed, Rule 1.17(c) ensures that the clients of a law practice maintain the freedom to do business with that practice (or take their business elsewhere) if it is sold.

QUESTION #140

Answer choice A is correct. This question tests Model Rule 6.3, under which a lawyer may serve as an officer of a legal services organization. Rule 6.3 permits a lawyer to maintain a leadership role in such an organization, even if the organization serves clients whose interests are adverse to the lawyer's clients. However, a lawyer serving in a leadership role in a legal services organization may not knowingly participate in a decision or action of the organization: "(a) if participating in the decision or action would be incompatible with the lawyer's obligations to a client under Rule 1.7 [governing conflicts of interest with a lawyer's current clients]; or (b) where the decision or action could have a material adverse effect on the representation of a client of the organization whose interests are adverse to a client of the lawyer." Under the facts of this question, the associate may remain on the board of directors, even though the organization represents clients whose interests are adverse to those of the associate's clients. However, the associate may not participate in the vote. If the organization is permitted to withdraw from representing its landlord-tenant clients, there is a substantial risk that those clients will be unable to get other representation and that their cases may be adversely affected. Because at least some of the organization's clients have interests adverse to those of the associate's clients, the associate should not participate in making this particular decision.

Answer choice B is incorrect because the associate may not knowingly participate in the decision if it will materially and adversely affect clients of the organization who have interests adverse to those of the associate's clients.

Answer choice C is incorrect because, as explained above, the attorney may serve on the organization's board of directors. For the same reason, answer choice D is incorrect; the associate has not violated any Rule of Professional Conduct simply by participating on the organization's board of directors.

QUESTION #141

Answer choice A is correct. This question tests Model Rules 7.5. Under Rule 7.5(c), if an attorney practicing in a firm takes public office, the firm may continue to use the public official's name in the firm name, provided that the attorney/public official continues to actively and regularly practice with the firm. Here, under state law, the lawyer cannot hold private employment. Therefore, the lawyer cannot continue to practice with the firm and consequently, he cannot be a named partner. Because the facts indicate that he cannot legally continue to practice with the firm, the firm must remove him as a named partner in order to comply with Rule 7.5(c).

Answer choice B is incorrect. As explained above, the partner may not practice law as long as he serves as the attorney general. Practicing as "of counsel" does not alter that requirement.

Answer choice C is incorrect because, although the partner cannot continue practicing law with the firm, his name must be removed from the firm name as set forth above.

Answer choice D is incorrect because, as explained above, the partner may not practice law as long as he serves as the attorney general.

QUESTION #142

Answer choice B is correct. The attorney would be subject to discipline if the attorney failed to adequately supervise the legal assistant. This question is testing Model Rule 5.3. Rule 5.3 addresses when an attorney may be subject to professional discipline for the conduct of a non-attorney assistant. Under Rule 5.3, a supervising lawyer must make reasonable efforts to ensure that the non-lawyer's conduct is compatible with the professional obligations of the lawyer. A lawyer will be responsible for conduct of such a person that would be a violation of the Rules if engaged in by a lawyer if one of the following two circumstances are present: 1) the lawyer orders or, with the knowledge of the specific conduct, ratifies the conduct involved; or 2) the lawyer is a partner or has comparable managerial authority in the law firm in which the person is employed, or has direct supervisory authority over the person, and knows of the conduct at a time when its consequences can be avoided or mitigated but fails to take reasonable remedial action. Thus, if the attorney failed to adequately supervise the legal assistant, the attorney would have violated the second prong of the test, and would be subject to discipline.

Answer choice A is incorrect because the theory of respondeat superior does not apply to professional discipline for the wrongful acts of a non-lawyer assistant. However, respondeat superior could apply to whether the attorney is subject to *civil liability* for the actions of the assistant.

Answer choice C is incorrect. Under rule 5.3, an attorney may be responsible for the negligence of a non-attorney if one of the two circumstances set forth above exist.

Answer choice D is incorrect because the negligence of the attorney is not *required* under the first prong of the test set forth above.

QUESTION #143

Answer choice C is correct. This question tests Model Rule of Professional Conduct ("MRPC") 6.2(c). Under Rule 6.2, a lawyer who has been asked to represent an indigent or unpopular person generally may not seek to avoid the representation unless good cause exists. Under Rule 6.2(c), good cause exists if "the client or the cause is so repugnant to the lawyer as to be likely to impair the client-lawyer relationship or the lawyer's ability to represent the client." Here, the facts indicate that, notwithstanding the lawyer's expertise in First Amendment matters, she finds the litigant's views so repugnant that she cannot bear the thought of representing him. In such a circumstance, good cause appears to exist for the lawyer to decline the representation.

Answer choice A is incorrect. Although a lawyer must generally accept an appointment by a tribunal, the lawyer may seek to avoid the appointment if good cause exists. MRPC 6.2, and the comments thereto, identify several circumstances creating good cause to decline a representation.

Answer choice B is incorrect because it is not supported by the facts in this question. Rule 6.2(b) notes that good cause to avoid a representation exists if "representing the client is likely to result in an unreasonable financial burden on the lawyer . . . ." Comment [2] to Rule 6.2 indicates that such a situation involves "a financial sacrifice so great as to be unjust." Although the lawyer in this question could seek to avoid the representation if it would create an unreasonable financial burden, nothing in the facts indicates that representing this particular litigant would create such a substantial burden.

Answer choice D is incorrect because although the lawyer's expertise may be relevant to whether the court ultimately permits her to decline the representation, she may nevertheless seek to decline the representation given her strong opposition to the litigant's views. *See* MRPC 6.2(c).

QUESTION #144

Answer choice A is correct. A lawyer is required to hold a client's money as a fiduciary, and he must keep such money separate from his own. *See* MRPC 1.15(a); Comment [1] to Rule 1.15. However, Rule 1.15(b) provides that it is permissible for a lawyer to pay bank service charges on a client trust account from the lawyer's own funds, "but only in an amount necessary for that purpose." Under the facts of this question, the lawyer has acted impermissibly by depositing more of his own money in the client trust account than is required to pay the bank's service charge.

Answer choice B is incorrect. Although it is generally impermissible to commingle a lawyer's funds with client funds, the Model Rules create an exception so that attorneys may pay bank service charges on client trust accounts. *See* MRPC 1.15(b). As Comment [2] to Rule 1.15 notes, a lawyer depositing his own funds into a client trust account to pay service charges must keep accurate records regarding which part of the funds belong to the lawyer.

Answer choice C is incorrect. That answer recognizes that a lawyer may commingle his funds with those of a client in very limited circumstances. *See* MRPC 1.15(b). However, Rule 1.15(b) limits the amount of funds a lawyer may commingle with client funds to the amount necessary to pay bank service charges; any further commingling is impermissible.

For the same reason, answer choice D is incorrect. A lawyer commingling his own funds with client funds to pay bank service charges is required to maintain accurate records identifying which portion of the funds belong to the lawyer. *See* Comment [2] to MRPC 1.15. However, the fact that such records are kept is irrelevant to whether a lawyer has impermissibly commingled funds by depositing more of his money in a client trust account than is needed to cover bank service charges.

QUESTION #145

Answer choice D is correct. This question tests Model Rule 5.4(c), which prohibits a lawyer from allowing a non-client who pays for the lawyer to represent a client to influence the lawyer's professional judgment with regard to the representation. Here, the lawyer has agreed to proceed in a manner that may be at odds with his client's – that is, the son's – stated interest. Thus, his agreement with the businessman runs afoul of Rule 5.4.

Answer choice A is incorrect. Regardless of whether the businessman is responsible for paying the lawyer, the lawyer is responsible for maintaining his professional independence in rendering services for his client – the son. *See* Rule 5.4(c).

Answer choice B is incorrect because the businessman's intent is irrelevant. Because the businessman's instruction to the lawyer has the effect of limiting the lawyer's ability to exercise his professional judgment, the lawyer may not agree to the instruction. *See* Rule 5.4(c).

Answer choice C is incorrect because the answer is not supported by the facts. Under Model Rule of Professional Conduct 1.5(d)(1), a lawyer may not charge a "fee in a domestic relations matter, the payment or amount of which is contingent upon the securing of a divorce or upon the amount of alimony or support, or property settlement in lieu thereof . . . ." However, nothing in the facts of this question indicates that the amount or payment of the lawyer's fee is contingent upon obtaining a certain outcome in the son's divorce proceedings.

QUESTION #146

Answer choice A is correct. Model Rule 1.5(d)(2) prohibits an attorney from charging a contingent fee for representing a defendant in a criminal case.

Answer choice B is incorrect. Even if the amount the attorney intends to charge the defendant for successfully representing him is reasonable under Model Rule 1.5(a), the agreement nevertheless runs afoul of the contingency fee prohibition in Rule 1.5(d)(2).

Answer choice C is incorrect because it overlooks the Rule 1.5(d)(2) prohibition against contingency fees for representing criminal defendants.

Answer choice D is incorrect. Although "[e]very lawyer has a professional responsibility to provide legal services to those unable to pay," Model Rule of Professional Conduct 6.1, the *pro bono publico* service requirement does not impose upon a lawyer the duty to represent at no charge every client of limited means who seeks representation. *But see* Model Rule 6.2 (governing a lawyer's responsibility to accept court-appointed cases). Indeed, Rule 6.1(b)(2) contemplates that a lawyer may take on a case "at a substantially reduced fee to persons of limited means." Here, the lawyer is not required to take on the young man's case *pro bono*. Nor, however, is she permitted to accept the representation on a contingency basis. *See* MRPC 1.5(d)(2).

QUESTION #147

Answer choice B is correct. This question tests Model Rule 7.2(b)(4), under which a lawyer may enter into a reciprocal referral agreement with a lawyer or non-lawyer, provided that: (i) the reciprocal referral agreement is not exclusive, and (ii) the client is informed of the existence and nature of the agreement. Under this agreement, the tax attorney and accountant refer clients to one another, but the agreement is not exclusive (the attorney refers clients to other accountants), and the attorney informs his clients of the referral agreement, even if he does not inform the clients of his personal friendship with the accountant. Thus, the agreement complies with Rule 7.2(b)(4).

Answer choice A is incorrect. Under Rule 7.2(b)(4), a reciprocal referral agreement is improper if the attorney involved does not inform clients of the existence and nature of the agreement. Although the attorney must tell clients that he and the accountant have an arrangement to refer clients to one another, nothing in Rule 7.2 requires the attorney to disclose his friendship with the accountant to his clients.

Answer choice C is incorrect. As noted above, Rule 7.2(b)(4) refers to agreements between lawyers as well as between a lawyer and a non-lawyer. However, as already noted, the reciprocal referral agreement between the tax attorney and the accountant is permissible under the Model Rules.

Answer choice D is incorrect. This answer reverses one of the requirements of Rule 7.2(b)(4) – that the referral agreement *not* be exclusive. As the facts of this question indicate, the tax attorney refers clients to several different accountants, so his agreement with his friend does not rule afoul of the Rules.

QUESTION #148

Answer choice B is correct. This question tests Model Rule 4.2, which governs an attorney's communications with other parties to a matter who are represented by counsel. Under that Rule, an attorney is prohibited from communicating about the subject of a case with a person he knows to be represented by another lawyer in the matter. As Comment [3] to Rule 4.2 notes, the Rule applies even though the represented person initiates the communication. Under the facts of this question, the business owner's attorney has been informed that the former employee is represented, and she has contacted him regarding the subject of the representation. Thus, the business owner's lawyer was required to immediately terminate the communication. *See* Comment [3] to Rule 4.2.

Answer choice A is incorrect. Under Rule 4.2 and the Comments thereto, the business owner's lawyer is prohibited from communicating with the former employee in any way regarding her case against the business owner. This includes even helpful advice. *See* Comments [2] and [3] to Rule 4.2.

Answer choice C is incorrect. As noted above, Rule 4.2 applies even if the represented person, not the lawyer, initiates the communication. *See* Comment [3] to Rule 4.2. Thus, the business owner's lawyer is still subject to discipline for communicating with the represented former employee, notwithstanding the fact that the former employee initiated the communication.

Answer choice D is incorrect. The fact that the business owner's lawyer did not give any legal advice to the former employee is irrelevant. Under Rule 4.2, he is still subject to discipline because he discussed the case with the former employee.

QUESTION #149

Answer choice D is correct. This question tests Model Rule 5.6, which generally prohibits a lawyer from agreeing to restrict his or her right to practice as part of the settlement of a case for a client. Because the proposed settlement in this case would require the family's lawyer to refrain from representing potential clients, it runs afoul of Rule 5.6. *See also* Comment [2] to Rule 5.6.

Answer choice A is incorrect because the value of the settlement to the lawyer's clients, though important, does not obviate the requirement that he not restrict his ability to represent potential clients. *See* MRPC 5.6. Answer choice B is incorrect for the same reason.

Answer choice C is incorrect, as it is not clearly dictated by any of the rules governing attorney conduct. Indeed, there may often be good reasons to settle rather than proceed to trial in a given case, notwithstanding the likelihood of a victory. The pertinent problem here, as discussed above, is the requirement that the family's lawyer not represent other plaintiffs in related litigation.

QUESTION #150

Answer choice B is correct. This question tests Model Rules 5.4(d)(1) and (2), which govern a lawyer's professional independence. Under that Rule, a lawyer may not practice in the form of a professional corporation or association authorized to practice law for profit if: "a nonlawyer is a corporate director or officer thereof or occupies the position of similar responsibility in any form of association other than a corporation," Rule 5.4(d)(2), or "a nonlawyer has the right to direct or control the professional judgment of a lawyer." Rule 5.4(d)(3). At a minimum, the attorney's agreement with his father violates Rule 5.4(d)(3) because the father, who is an accountant, not a lawyer, has the right to control the attorney's professional judgment as to whether to take the case. Further, it seems that their arrangement also violates Rule 5.4(d)(2), as the father's role is akin to that of a manager or officer.

Answer choice A is incorrect. Although this answer choice recognizes that, pursuant to Rule 5.4(d)(1), a non-lawyer may not own an interest in a firm – a condition distinguishable from the father holding a financial debt owed by the firm – it ignores those aspects of the agreement between the attorney and his father that violate Rules 5.4(d)(2) and (3).

Answer choice C is incorrect because the duration of the father's veto power is irrelevant. Rule 5.4(d)(3) speaks in absolute terms: a lawyer must not give a non-lawyer the right to control his professional judgment.

Answer choice D is incorrect. Although this answer choice recognizes that a lawyer and non-lawyer may not form a partnership if the partnership practices law in any way, *see* Rule 5.4(b), and that the arrangement between the attorney and his father does not violate that Rule, it ignores those aspects of the agreement between the attorney and his father that violate Rules 5.4(d)(2) and (3).

18822235R00089

Made in the USA
San Bernardino, CA
31 January 2015